CREATING A NEW CIVILIZATION

THE POLITICS OF THE THIRD WAVE

CREATING
A NEW
CIVILIZATION

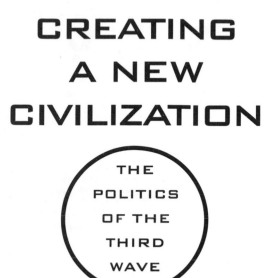

THE
POLITICS
OF THE
THIRD
WAVE

ALVIN AND HEIDI TOFFLER

FOREWORD BY NEWT GINGRICH

Turner Publishing, Inc.
ATLANTA

BOOKS BY ALVIN AND HEIDI TOFFLER
THE CULTURE CONSUMERS
FUTURE SHOCK
THE ECO-SPASM REPORT
THE THIRD WAVE
PREVIEWS AND PREMISES
THE ADAPTIVE CORPORATION
POWERSHIFT
WAR AND ANTI-WAR

BOOKS EDITED BY ALVIN AND HEIDI TOFFLER
THE FUTURISTS
LEARNING FOR TOMORROW
THE SCHOOLHOUSE AND THE CITY

An earlier edition of this book was published in 1994 by The Progress & Freedom Foundation.

Grateful acknowledgment is made to the following for permission
to reprint previously published material:

The Third Wave by Alvin Toffler. © 1980 by Alvin Toffler.
Reprinted by permission of Bantam Books.

Powershift by Alvin Toffler. © 1990 by Alvin and Heidi Toffler.
Reprinted by permission of Bantam Books.

War and Anti-War by Alvin and Heidi Toffler. © 1993 by Alvin Toffler and Heidi Toffler.
Reprinted by permission of Little Brown and Company.

Library of Congress Cataloging-in-Publication Data
Toffler, Alvin.
    Creating a new civilization: the politics of the Third Wave/by
Alvin and Heidi Toffler; foreword by Newt Gingrich.—1st ed.
        p. cm.
    ISBN: 1-57036-224-6 (hardcover) ISBN: 1-57036-223-8 (paperback)
    1. Social history—1945– 2. Social change. 3. Forecasting.
    4. Civilization, Modern—1950– I. Toffler, Heidi, 1929–   .
    II. Title.
HN17.5.T636   1995
303.4973—dc20   95–795
                                                             CIP

PUBLISHED BY TURNER PUBLISHING, INC.
A SUBSIDIARY OF TURNER BROADCASTING SYSTEM, INC.
1050 TECHWOOD DRIVE, N.W.
ATLANTA, GEORGIA 30318

DISTRIBUTED BY ANDREWS AND MCMEEL
A UNIVERSAL PRESS SYNDICATE COMPANY
4900 MAIN STREET
KANSAS CITY, MISSOURI 64112

FIRST EDITION
10 9 8 7 6 5 4 3 2 1

PRINTED IN THE U.S.A.

CONTENTS

PREFACE

America faces a convergence of crises unmatched since its earliest days. Its family system is in crisis, but so is its health system, its urban systems, its value system and above all, its political system, which for all practical purposes has lost the confidence of the people. Why should these—and many other crises—all strike at approximately the same time in our history? Are they evidence of terminal decay in America? Are we at the "end of history"?

These pages tell a different story. America's crises stem not from its failure but from its earlier successes. Rather than the end of history, we are at the end of *pre*-history.

Ever since 1970, when our book *Future Shock* introduced the concept of the "general crisis of industrial society," our smokestack industries have been laying off masses of manual workers. Precisely as first forecast in that book, our family structure has fractured, our mass media have de-massified, and our life styles and values have diversified. America has become a radically different place.

This explains why all the old forms of political analysis no longer apply. Terms like "right-wing" and "left-wing" or "liberal" and conservative" are drained of their familiar meanings. In Russia these days, we speak of Communists as "conservatives"

7

and reformers as "radicals." In the U.S., economic liberals may be social conservatives and vice versa. "Left-wing" Ralph Nader unites with "right-wing" Pat Buchanan to oppose NAFTA.

Even more jarring and significant, however, is the growing transfer of political power away from our formal political structures—the Congress, the White House, the government agencies and political parties—to electronically-linked grassroots groups and to the media.

These and other massive changes in American political life cannot be explained in political terms alone. They are related to equally deep changes in family life, in business, in technology, culture and values. To govern in this period of high-speed change, disillusionment, and almost fratricidal conflict in society, we need a coherent approach to the twenty-first century. This book presents a powerful new framework for change. Once this framework is understood, we can take practical steps to shape the even greater changes that lie ahead—to direct them, rather than allow ourselves to be victimized by them.

A defining characteristic of change today is its pace. Events move swiftly, and acceleration affects everything—even, it seems, the fate of books.

Barely a month after this volume was first issued in a limited educational edition by the Progress and Freedom Foundation in October 1994, an election propelled Newt Gingrich to the office of Speaker of the U.S. House of Representatives. The resultant furor swept this book onto the front pages and television screens of the nation. Not only does this book carry a foreword by Gingrich, but it appears on a "reading list" that he recommended to members of Congress and to the nation, alongside *The Federalist Papers*, the works of DeTocqueville, and other classics of political philosophy.

Moreover, in speech after speech and in one press conference after another, Gingrich has referred to our 1980 work, *The Third*

Wave, from which parts of this book are drawn, as "one of the seminal works of our time."

One result of the election and the appearance of this book has been an unprecedented clamor by the media for information about our friendship with Newt Gingrich. After all, we have been publicly identified with many political positions that are at odds with his. How strange, reporters repeatedly say, that social thinkers and futurists like you should have anything to do with a conservative politician like Gingrich. Don't all conservatives want a return to the past?

The answer is no—not necessarily. It's not that simple.

To those who wonder why Gingrich urges Americans to read our books—the work of authors who oppose prayer in schools and who are pro-choice—and to those who wonder why we proudly claim Gingrich and his wife Marianne as personal friends, this brief introduction to our ideas is the best answer.

We have known Newt Gingrich for almost a quarter century. Shortly after we published *Future Shock* in 1970, a young teaching assistant with longish hair and Elvis-proportion sideburns flew up from Georgia to hear us speak at an educational conference in Chicago. He was impressed by our book and introduced himself to us. It was years before he first ran for political office.

In 1975 at the request of Congressional Democrats, we organized a conference on futurism and "anticipatory democracy" for senators and members of the House. We invited Newt Gingrich, probably the only Republican among the many futurists we knew. He attended.

That conference led to the creation of the Congressional Clearinghouse on the Future, a group eventually cochaired by a young senator named Al Gore, now vice president and the man who has placed the need for an information infrastructure on the national agenda.

In the intervening years we have developed a close personal relationship with the Gingriches, and have argued endlessly not simply about specific political issues but about broad social theory, philosophy, world events, and the future. Often when our arguments reach a high decibel level, we find ourselves bursting into laughter. Caricatured by the media as some kind of conservative Savonarola, Gingrich has a trait fanatics typically lack, a keen sense of humor.

Our personal relationship with the Gingriches has been warm and our intellectual relationship has been wide ranging and combative. Newt is interested in everything—the space program, dinosaurs, the daily troubles of a young district attorney, learning theory, military history, Hollywood movies, and of course politics, politics, and still more politics. So we have plenty to argue about. And while our arguments do not necessarily end in agreement, they do sharpen our minds.

Newt once said to us, as we are sure he has said to others, that we might easily agree with eighty percent of his views and simply *detest* the other twenty percent. Since then the percentage has risen and fallen sharply from time to time.

If Gingrich is not the single smartest and most successful intellectual in American politics, he is surely one of a very small group. A former professor of European history and environmental studies, he thinks in long sweeps of time and regularly infuses his speech with words like "civilization" and "revolution." But unlike most historians who look only backward, and politicians who look no farther forward than the next election, Gingrich is exactly what he says he is—a revolutionary and a conservative futurist. As a futurist he thinks strategically and looks thirty and forty years ahead, even when he is engaged in immediate tactical struggles.

Thus any voter, citizen, reporter or politician who imagines that Gingrich is just another "pol" is buying into a sound bite image of him that distorts the reality. The fact is, whether or not you like what he has to say (and he sometimes blurts words he is sorry for the next day), Gingrich has thought very long and hard about what he is doing and where he thinks America should go in the first quarter of the next century.

As the authors of *Creating a New Civilization*, we should state for the record that we are neither Republicans nor Democrats. And we not only consult with Gingrich on occasion, but were delighted when, after the recent election, the Democratic leadership in the Congress began to express renewed interest in our ideas. They invited us to discuss the political meaning of the Third Wave and began to circulate copies of this book among themselves. Of course they know of our long-standing friendship with Gingrich, and Newt, when told we are talking to Democrats, said "that's terrific." The future shouldn't be the property of any one party.

This brief book will explain why, in our opinion, the time has come for the next great step forward in American politics. It is not a matter of Democrats versus Republicans, or of left and right, or even of liberals and conservatives, but something more significant. What is needed, we believe, is a clear distinction between rear-guard politicians who wish to preserve or restore an unworkable past, and those who are ready to make the transition to what we call a "Third Wave" information-age society.

If nothing else, global competition means we cannot go back to the conformity, uniformity, bureaucracy and brute force economy of the assembly-line era. But the Third Wave is not just a matter of technology and economics. It involves morality, culture and ideas as well as institutions and political structure. It implies, in short, a true transformation in human affairs.

Just as the industrial revolution destroyed or rendered irrelevant many of the political structures that preceded it, the knowledge revolution—and the Third Wave of change it has launched—will do the same to America and many other countries. Political parties and movements that recognize this historical fact will survive and shape the future for our children. Those that fail to do so will swirl down the storm drain of history.

ALVIN AND HEIDI TOFFLER
JANUARY 1995

A CITIZEN'S GUIDE TO THE TWENTY-FIRST CENTURY

BY NEWT GINGRICH

The 1990s have initiated a wave of political and governmental change of historic proportions: the collapse of the Soviet Empire, the replacement of the post-World War II Italian political structure, the virtual elimination of the Canadian governing party in the 1993 elections (they dropped from 153 seats to 2 in the Parliament), the collapse of the Japanese Liberal Democratic Party after a forty-year virtual monopoly of power (and the rise of a new reform movement), the rise of Ross Perot and the United We Stand movement and the election of 1994 in America. Again and again there are startling changes under way in politics and government.

Politicians, columnists and academics all seem confused by the scale of change. There is an inevitable focus on the pain of those who have been dominant and the disorientation of those who have been powerful. The agony of the past is outweighing the promise of the future. This is an old phenomenon. Huizenga's *The Waning of the Middle Ages* made this point about the Renaissance: looking back in history, what seems to us a brilliant, exciting period of innovation seemed to its contemporaries a terrifying collapse of the existing order. Similarly, the collapse of Confucian China from the 1850s on was seen as a terrifying decline of order and stability rather than the

13

precursor of a new, more productive and more open future.

Alvin and Heidi Toffler have given us the key to viewing current disarray within the positive framework of a dynamic, exciting future. They have been teaching, speaking and writing about the future for a quarter century. The title of their first bestseller, *Future Shock* (1970), became a universal term for the scale of change we are living through. (It was an even bigger bestseller in Japan than the United States on a per capita basis.) *Future Shock* called attention to the acceleration of change that was threatening to overwhelm people everywhere and the way in which it often disoriented individuals, businesses, communities and governments.

If *Future Shock* had been their only work, the Tofflers would have been recognized as important commentators on the human condition. However, their next major work, *The Third Wave*, was an even more important contribution to understanding our times. In *The Third Wave*, the Tofflers moved from observation to creating a predictive framework. They placed the information revolution in historical perspective, comparing it with two other great transformations, the agricultural revolution and the industrial revolution. According to the Tofflers, we are feeling the impact of the third great wave of change in history, and we are, as a result, in the process of creating a new civilization.

The Tofflers correctly understand that development and distribution of information has now become the central productivity and power activity of the human race. From world financial markets to the worldwide, twenty-four-hour-a-day distribution of news via CNN to the breakthroughs of the biological revolution and their impact on health and agricultural production—on virtually every front we see the information revolution changing the fabric, pace and substance of our lives.

Because *The Third Wave* makes sense of this transformation, it has had a powerful impact on the strategies of business and political leaders outside the United States in China, Japan, Singapore and other fast-rising regions that now focus on high-tech, information-intensive development. In the United States too, many business leaders have been influenced by the book, as they have restructured their organizations to prepare for the twenty-first century.

One of the most important and successful applications of the Third Wave model occurred when General Donn Starry, commander of the U.S. Army Training and Doctrine Command (TRADOC), read *The Third Wave* in the early 1980s and decided the Tofflers were correct in their analysis of the future. As a result, the Tofflers were invited to Fort Monroe, the headquarters of TRADOC, where they shared the Third Wave model with doctrine developers throughout the Army. The Tofflers describe this model brilliantly in their recent book *War and Anti-War*. I know how influential the concept of a Third Wave information revolution was in the Army doctrine development effort from 1979 to 1982 because I spent a lot of time as a junior congressman working with General Starry and General Morelli (now deceased) developing the concepts which became Air/Land Battle.

The new Army doctrine led to a more flexible, fast-paced, decentralized, information-rich system which assessed the battlefield, focused resources and utilized well-trained but very decentralized leadership to overwhelm an industrial-era opponent.

In 1991 the world witnessed the first war between Third Wave military systems and an obsolete Second Wave military machine. Desert Storm was a one-sided annihilation of the Iraqis by the Americans and their allies largely because Third Wave systems proved overwhelmingly that sophisticated Second Wave anti-aircraft systems were useless against Third Wave stealth aircraft. Entrenched Second Wave armies were simply outmaneuvered and annihilated when faced with Third Wave information systems for targeting and logistics. The result was a campaign as decisive as the defeat of the First Wave forces of the Mahdi of Omdurman by the Second Wave Anglo-Egyptian army in 1898.

Despite evidence that something radically new is happening in politics, in economics, in society and in warfare, there is still remarkably little appreciation of how crucial the Tofflers' insight is. Most American politicians, reporters and editorial writers have ignored the implications of *The Third Wave*. There is even less systematic effort to integrate the concept of a Third Wave of human change into policy proposals, political campaigns and the operations of government. This failure to apply the Toffler Third Wave model has kept our politics trapped in frustration, negativism, cynicism and despair.

The gap between objective changes in the world at large and the stagnation of politics and government is undermining the very fabric of our political system. Aside from the Third Wave concept there is no effective system of analysis which makes sense of the frustration and confusion which characterizes politics and government virtually everywhere in the industrial world. There is no language to communicate the problems we face, no vision to outline the future towards which we should strive, and no program to help accelerate and make easier the transition.

This is not a new problem. I first began working with the Tofflers in the early 1970s on a concept called anticipatory democracy. I was then a young assistant professor at West Georgia State College, and I was fascinated with the intersection of history and the future which is the essence of politics and government at its best. For twenty years we have worked to develop a future-conscious politics and popular understanding that would make it easier for America to make the transition from the Second Wave civilization—which is clearly dying—to the emerging, but in many ways undefined and not fully understood Third Wave civilization.

The process has been more frustrating and the progress much slower than I would have guessed two decades ago. Yet despite the frustrations, the development of a Third Wave political and governmental system is so central to the future of freedom and the future of America that it must be undertaken.

While I am a Republican leader in the Congress, I do not believe Republicans or the Congress have a monopoly on solving problems and helping America make the transformation necessary to enter the Third Wave information revolution. Democratic mayors like Norquist in Milwaukee and Rendel in Philadelphia are making real breakthroughs at the city level. Some of the best of Vice President Gore's efforts to reinvent government nibble in the right direction (although timidly and without making a decisive breakthrough).

The reality is that transformation is going on everyday in the private sector among entrepreneurs and with citizens who are inventing new things and creating new solutions because bureaucracy doesn't stop them.

On January 5, 1995, the Third Wave came to American democracy in the form of "Thomas," the Library of Congress's on-line system that allows every citizen to access copies of legislation, committee reports and other congressional documents. During its first four days of operation, 28,000 individuals and 2,500 institutions used Thomas to download 175,132 documents. In fact, more citizens accessed Thomas over a twenty-four-hour period than normally use the Library of Congress in a week.

Like Thomas, this book is an effort to empower citizens like yourself to truly take the leap and begin to invent a Third Wave civilization. I believe that if you read through the Tofflers' remarkable contribution to the great transformation, underline the parts you find useful, wander around your community looking for kindred spirits, and begin to develop a few small projects, you will be shocked in a few years at how much you have accomplished.

NEWT GINGRICH
JANUARY 1995

SUPER STRUGGLE

A new civilization is emerging in our lives, and blind men everywhere are trying to suppress it. This new civilization brings with it new family styles, changed ways of working, loving, and living, a new economy, new political conflicts, and beyond all this an altered consciousness as well.

Humanity faces a quantum leap forward. It faces the deepest social upheaval and creative restructuring of all time. Without clearly recognizing it, we are engaged in building a remarkable new civilization from the ground up. This is the meaning of the Third Wave.

Until now the human race has undergone two great waves of change, each one largely obliterating earlier cultures or civilizations and replacing them with ways of life inconceivable to those who came before. The First Wave of change—the agricultural revolution —took thousands of years to play itself out. The Second Wave—the rise of industrial civilization—took a mere three hundred years. Today history is even more accelerative, and it is likely that the Third Wave will sweep across history and complete itself in a few decades. Those of us who happen to share the planet at this explosive moment will therefore feel the full impact of the Third Wave in our own lifetimes.

The Third Wave brings with it a genuinely new way of life

based on diversified, renewable energy sources; on methods of production that make most factory assembly lines obsolete; on new, non-nuclear families; on a novel institution that might be called the "electronic cottage;" and on radically changed schools and corporations of the future. The emergent civilization writes a new code of behavior for us and carries us beyond standardization, synchronization and centralization, beyond the concentration of energy, money and power.

This new civilization has its own distinctive world outlook; its own ways of dealing with time, space, logic and causality. And, its own principles for the politics of the future.

THE REVOLUTIONARY PREMISE

Two apparently contrasting images of the future grip the popular imagination today. Most people, to the extent that they bother to think about the future at all, assume the world they know will last indefinitely. They find it difficult to imagine a truly different way of life for themselves, let alone a totally new civilization. Of course, they recognize that things are changing. But they assume today's changes will somehow pass them by and that nothing will shake the familiar economic framework and political structure. They confidently expect the future to continue as the present.

Recent events have severely shaken this confident image of the future. A bleaker vision has become increasingly popular. Large numbers of people fed on a steady diet of bad news, disaster movies and nightmare scenarios issued by prestigious think tanks have apparently concluded that today's society cannot be projected into the future because there is no future. For them, Armageddon is only minutes away. The Earth is racing toward its final cataclysmic shudder.

Our argument is based on what we call the "revolutionary premise." It assumes that, even though the decades immediately ahead are likely to be filled with upheavals, turbulence, perhaps even widespread violence, we will not totally destroy ourselves. It assumes that the jolting changes we are now experiencing are not chaotic or random but they, in fact, form a sharp, clearly discernible pattern. It assumes, moreover, that these changes are cumulative—that they add up to a giant transformation in the way we live, work, play and think, and that a sane and desirable future is possible. In short, what follows begins with the premise that what is happening now is nothing less than a global revolution, a quantum leap.

Put differently, it flows from the assumption that we are the final generation of an old civilization and the first generation of a new one, that much of our personal confusion, anguish, and disorientation can be traced directly to the conflict within us and within our political institutions, between the dying Second Wave civilization and the emergent Third Wave civilization that is thundering in to take its place.

When we finally understand this, many seemingly senseless events become suddenly comprehensible. Broad patterns of change begin to emerge clearly. Action for survival becomes possible and plausible again. In short, the revolutionary premise liberates our intellect and will.

THE LEADING EDGE

One powerful new approach might be called social "wavefront" analysis. It looks at history as a succession of rolling waves of change and asks where the leading edge of each wave is carrying us. It focuses our attention not so much on the continuities of history (important as they are) as on the discontinuities, on innovations and breakpoints. It identifies key change patterns as they emerge so that we can influence them.

It begins with the very simple idea that the rise of agriculture was the first turning point in human social development and that the industrial revolution was the second great breakthrough. It views each of these not as a discrete, one-time event but as a wave of change moving at a certain velocity.

Before the First Wave of change, most humans lived in small, often migratory groups and fed them selves by foraging, fishing, hunting or herding. At some point, roughly ten millennia ago, the agricultural revolution began and crept slowly across the planet spreading villages, settlements, cultivated land and a new way of life.

This First Wave of change had not yet exhausted itself by the end of the seventeenth century when the industrial revolution broke over Europe and unleashed the second great wave of planetary change. This new process began moving much more rapidly across nations and continents. Thus, two separate and distinct change processes were rolling across the earth simultaneously, but at different speeds.

Today the First Wave has virtually subsided. Only a few tiny pre-agrarian populations in South America or Papua New Guinea, for example, remain to be reached by agriculture. The force of this great First Wave has basically been spent.

Meanwhile, the Second Wave, having revolutionized life in Europe, North America and some other parts of the globe in a few short centuries, continues to spread, as many countries—until now basically agricultural—scramble to build steel mills, auto plants, textile factories, railroads and food-processing plants. The momentum of industrialization is still felt. This Second Wave has not entirely spent its force.

But even as this process continues, another, even more important, has begun. For as the tide of industrialism peaked in the decades after World War II, a little-understood Third Wave began to surge across the earth, transforming everything it touched.

Many countries, therefore, are feeling the simultaneous impact of two, even three, quite different waves of change, all moving at different rates of speed and with different degrees of force behind them.

For our purposes we shall consider the First Wave era to have begun sometime around 8000 B.C. and to have dominated the earth unchallenged until sometime around A.D. 1650–1750. From this moment on, the First Wave lost momentum as the Second Wave picked up steam. Industrial civilization, the product of this Second Wave, then dominated the planet in its turn until it, too, crested. This latest historical turning point arrived in the United States during the decade beginning about 1955—a decade that saw white-collar and service workers outnumber blue-collar workers for the first time. This was the same decade that saw the widespread introduction of the computer, commercial jet travel, the birth-control pill and other high-impact innovations. It was precisely during this decade that the Third Wave began to gather its force in the United States. Since then it has arrived at slightly different dates in most of the other industrial nations. Today all high-technology nations are reeling from the collision between the Third Wave and the obsolete, encrusted economies and institutions of the Second.

Understanding this is the secret to making sense of much of the political and social conflict we see around us.

WAVES OF THE FUTURE

Whenever a single wave of change predominates in any given society, the pattern of future development is relatively easy to discern. Writers, artists, journalists and others discover the "wave of the future." Thus, in nineteenth-century Europe many thinkers, business leaders, politicians and ordinary people held a clear, basically correct image of the future. They sensed that history was moving toward the ultimate triumph of industrialism over premechanized agriculture, and they foresaw with considerable accuracy many of the changes that the

Second Wave would bring with it: more powerful technologies, bigger cities, faster transport, mass education and the like.

This clarity of vision had direct political effects. Parties and political movements were able to triangulate with respect to the future. Preindustrial agricultural interests organized a rearguard action against encroaching industrialism, against "big business," against "union bosses," against "sinful cities." Labor and management grappled for control of the main levers of the emergent industrial society. Ethnic and racial minorities, defining their rights in terms of an improved role in the industrial world, demanded access to jobs, corporate positions, urban housing, better wages and mass public education.

This industrial vision of the future had important psychological effects as well. The shared image of an industrial future tended to define options, to give individuals a sense not merely of who or what they were but of what they were likely to become. It provided a degree of stability and a sense of self, even in the midst of extreme social change.

In contrast, when a society is struck by two or more giant waves of change and none is yet clearly dominant, the image of the future is fractured. It be comes extremely difficult to sort out the meaning of the changes and conflicts that arise. The collision of wave fronts creates a raging ocean full of clashing currents, eddies and maelstroms which conceal the deeper, more important historic tides.

In the United States—and in many other countries—the collision of Second and Third Waves creates social tensions, dangerous conflicts and strange new political wave fronts that cut across the usual divisions of class, race, sex or party. This collision makes a shambles of traditional political vocabularies and makes it very difficult to separate progressives from reactionaries, friends from enemies. All the old polarizations and coalitions break up.

The apparent incoherence of political life is mirrored in personality disintegration. Psychotherapists and gurus do a land-office business, people wander aimlessly amid competing therapies. They slip into cults and covens or, alternatively, into a pathological privatism, convinced that reality is absurd, insane or meaningless. Life may indeed be absurd in some large, cosmic sense. But this hardly proves that there is no pattern in today's events. In fact, there is a distinct, hidden order that becomes detectable as soon as we learn to distinguish Third Wave changes from those associated with a diminishing Second Wave.

The crosscurrents created by these waves of change are reflected in our work, family life, sexual attitudes and personal morality. They show up in life-styles and voting behavior. For in our personal lives and political acts, whether we know it or not, most of us in the rich countries are essentially Second Wave people committed to maintaining a dying order, Third Wave people constructing a radically different tomorrow or a confused, self-canceling mixture of the two.

The conflict between Second and Third Wave groupings is, in fact, the central political tension cutting through our society today. The more basic political question, as we shall see, is not who controls the last days of industrial society but who shapes the new civilization rapidly rising to replace it. On one side are the partisans of the industrial past; on the other, growing millions who recognize that the most urgent problems of the world can no longer be resolved within the frame work of an industrial order. This conflict is the "super struggle" for tomorrow.

This confrontation between the vested interests of the Second Wave and the people of the Third Wave already runs like an electric current through the political life of every nation. Even in the nonindustrial countries of the world, all the old battle lines have been forcibly redrawn by the arrival of the Third Wave. The old war of agricultural, often feudal interests against industrializing elites, either capitalist or socialist, takes on a new dimension in light of the coming obsolescence of industrialism. Now that Third Wave civilization is making its appearance, does rapid industrialization imply liberation from neocolonialism and poverty, or does it, in fact, guarantee permanent dependency?

It is only against this wide-screen background that we can begin to make sense of the headlines, to sort out our priorities, to frame sensible strategies for the control of change in our lives. Once we realize that a bitter struggle is now raging between those who seek to preserve industrialism and those who seek to supplant it, we have a new tool for changing that world.

To use this tool, however, we must be able to distinguish clearly those changes that extend the old industrial civilization from those which facilitate the arrival of the new. We must, in short, understand both the old and the new, the Second Wave industrial system into which so many of us were born and the Third Wave civilization that we and our children will inhabit.

A CLASH OF CIVILIZATIONS

It has belatedly begun to dawn on people that industrial civilization is coming to an end. Its unraveling—already evident in 1970 when we wrote about the "general crisis of industrialism" in *Future Shock*—brings with it the threat of more, not fewer, wars—wars of a new type.

Because massive changes in society cannot occur without conflict, we believe the metaphor of history as "waves" of change is more dynamic and revealing than talk about a transition to "post-modernism." Waves are dynamic. When waves crash in on one another, powerful crosscurrents are unleashed. When waves of history collide, whole civilizations clash. And that sheds light on much that otherwise seems senseless or random in today's world.

The *wave theory of conflict* tells us that the main conflict we face is not between Islam and the West or "the rest against the West," as recently suggested by Samuel Huntington. Nor is America in decline, as Paul Kennedy declares. Nor are we, in Francis Fukuyama's phrase, facing the "end of history." The deepest economic and strategic change of all is the coming division of the world into three distinct, differing, and potentially clashing civilizations that cannot be mapped using the conventional definitions.

First Wave civilization was and still is inescapably attached to the land. Whatever local form it takes, whatever language its people speak, whatever its religion or belief system, it is a product of the agricultural revolution. Even today, multitudes live and die scrabbling at the unyielding soil as their ancestors did centuries ago.

Second Wave civilization's origins are in dispute. But life did not fundamentally change for large numbers of people until, roughly speaking, three hundred years ago. That was when Newtonian science first arose. It is when the steam engine was first put to economic use and the first factories began to proliferate in Britain, France and Italy. Peasants began moving into the cities. Daring new ideas began to circulate: the idea of progress, the odd doctrine of individual rights, the Rousseauian notion of a social contract, secularism, the separation of church and state, and the novel idea that leaders should be chosen by popular will, not divine right.

Driving many of these changes was a new way of creating wealth—factory production. And before long many different elements came together to form a system: mass production, mass consumption, mass education, mass media all linked together and served by specialized institutions—schools, corporations, and political parties. Even family structure changed from the large, agrarian-style household in which several generations lived together to the small, stripped-down nuclear family typical of industrial societies.

To the people actually experiencing these many changes, life must have seemed chaotic. Yet the changes were, in fact, all closely interrelated. They were merely steps toward the full development of what we came to call modernity—mass-industrial society, the civilization of the Second Wave.

That term, "civilization," may sound pretentious, especially to many American ears, but no other term is sufficiently all-embracing to include such varied matters as technology, family life, religion, culture, politics, business, hierarchy, leadership, values, sexual morality and epistemology. Swift and radical changes are occurring in every one of these dimensions of society. Change so many social, technological and cultural elements at once and you create not just a transition but a transformation, not just a new society but the beginnings, at least, of a totally new civilization.

This new civilization entered history with a roar in Western Europe, fiercely resisted at every step.

THE MASTER CONFLICT

In every industrializing country bitter, often bloody battles broke out between Second Wave industrial and commercial groups and First Wave landowners in alliance very often with the church (itself a great landowner). Masses of peasants were forced off the land to provide workers for the new "satanic mills" and factories that multiplied over the landscape.

Strikes and rebellions, civil insurrections, border disputes and nationalist uprisings erupted as the war between First and Second Wave interest became the master conflict—the central tensions from which other conflicts derived. This pattern was repeated in almost every industrializing country. In the United States it required a terrible Civil War for the industrial-commercial interest of the North to vanquish the agrarian elites of the South. Only a few years later, the Meiji Revolution broke out in Japan, and once more Second Wave Modernizers triumphed over the First Wave traditionalists.

The spread of Second Wave civilization, with its strange new way of making wealth, destabilized relationships between countries as well, creating power vacuums and power shifts.

Industrial civilization, the product of the great Second Wave of change, took root most rapidly on the northern shores of the great Atlantic Basin. As the Atlantic powers industrialized, they needed markets and cheap raw materials from distant regions. The advanced Second Wave powers thus waged wars of colonial conquest and came to dominate the remaining First Wave states and tribal units all over Asia and Africa.

It was the master conflict again—Second Wave industrial powers versus First Wave agrarian powers—but this time on a global rather than domestic scale, and it was this struggle that basically determined the shape of the world until recent times. It set the frame within which most wars took place.

Tribal and territorial wars between different primitive and agricultural groups continued as they had throughout previous millennia. But these were of limited importance and often merely weakened both sides, making them easy prey for the colonizing forces of industrial civilization. This happened, for example, in southern Africa, as Cecil Rhodes and his armed agents seized vast territories from tribal and agrarian groups busy fighting one another with primitive weapons. Elsewhere, too, many seemingly unconnected wars around the world were, in fact, expressions of the main global conflict not between competing states but competing civilizations.

Yet the very biggest and most murderous wars during the industrial age were intra-industrial—wars that pitted Second Wave nations like Germany and Britain against one another, as each one struggled for global dominance while keeping the world's First Wave populations in their subordinate place.

The ultimate result was a clear division. The industrial era bisected the world into a dominant and dominating Second Wave civilization and scores of sullen but subordinate First Wave colonies. Many of us grew up in this world divided between First and Second Wave civilizations. And it was perfectly clear which one held power.

Today, the lineup of world civilizations is different. We are speeding toward a totally different structure of power that will create not a world cut in two but sharply divided into three contrasting and competing civilizations—the first still symbolized by the hoe, the second by the assembly line, and the third by the computer.

In this trisected world the First Wave sector supplies agricultural and mineral resources, the Second Wave sector provides cheap labor and does the mass production, and a rapidly expanding Third Wave sector rises to dominance based on the new ways in which it creates and exploits knowledge.

Third Wave nations sell information and innovation, management, culture and pop culture, advanced technology, software, education, training, medical care and financial and other services to the world. One of those services might well also turn out to be military protection based on its command of superior Third Wave forces. (That is, in effect, what the high-tech nations provided for Kuwait and Saudi Arabia in the Gulf War.)

DE-MASSIFIED SOCIETIES

The Second Wave created mass societies that reflected and required mass production. In Third Wave, brain-based economies, mass production (which could almost be considered the defining mark of industrial society) is already an outmoded form. De-massified production—short runs of highly customized products—is the new cutting edge of manufacture. Mass marketing gives way to market segmentation and "particle marketing," paralleling the change in production. Old industrial-style behemoths collapse of their own mass and face destruction. Labor unions in the mass manufacturing sector shrink. The mass media are de-massified in parallel with production, and giant TV net works shrivel as new channels proliferate. The family system, too, becomes de-massified: the nuclear family, once the modern standard, becomes a minority form while single-parent households, remarried couples, childless families and live-alones proliferate.

The entire structure of society, therefore, changes as the homogeneity of Second Wave society is replaced by the heterogeneity of Third Wave civilization. Massification gives way to de-massification.

In turn, the very complexity of the new system requires more and more information exchange among its units—companies, government agencies, hospitals, associations, other institutions, even individuals. This creates a ravenous need for computers, digital telecommunications networks and new media.

Simultaneously, the pace of technological change, transactions and daily life speeds up. In fact, Third Wave economies operate at speeds so accelerated that their premodern suppliers can barely keep pace. Moreover, as information increasingly substitutes for bulk raw materials, labor and other resources, Third Wave countries become less dependent on First Wave or Second Wave partners, except for markets. More and more they do business with each other. Eventually, their highly capitalized, knowledge-based technology will take over many tasks now done by the cheap-labor countries and actually do them faster, better—and more cheaply.

Put differently, these changes threaten to slash many of the existing economic links between the rich economies and the poor.

Complete de-coupling is impossible. It is not possible to stop pollution, disease and immigration from penetrating the borders of the Third Wave countries. Nor can the rich nations survive if the poor wage ecological war on them by manipulating their environment in ways that damage everyone. For these reasons, tensions between the Third Wave civilization and the two older forms of civilizations will continue to rise, and the new civilization may well fight to establish global hegemony, just as

Second Wave modernizers did with respect to the First Wave premodern societies in centuries past.

Once this concept of the clash of civilizations is grasped, it helps us make sense of many seemingly odd phenomena—today's flaring nationalisms, for example. Nationalism is the ideology of the nation-state, which is a product of the industrial revolution. Thus, as First Wave, or agrarian, societies seek to start or complete their industrialization, they demand the trappings of nationhood. Former Soviet republics like the Ukraine or Estonia or Georgia fiercely insist on self-determination, and demand yesterday's marks of modernity—the flags, armies and currencies that defined the nation-state during the Second Wave, or industrial, era.

It is hard for many in the high-tech world to comprehend the motivations of ultra-nationalists. Their puffed-up patriotism strikes many as amusing. It calls to mind the land of Freedonia in the Marx Brothers' movie *Duck Soup*, which satirized national superiority as two fictional nations went to war.

By contrast, it is incomprehensible to nationalists how some countries allow others to invade their sacred independence. Yet the "globalization" of business and finance required by the advancing Third Wave economies routinely punctures the national "sovereignty" the new nationalists hold so dear.

As economies are transformed by the Third Wave, they are compelled to surrender part of their sovereignty and to accept increasing economic and cultural intrusions from one another. Thus, while poets and intellectuals of economically backward regions write national anthems, poets and intellectuals of Third Wave states sing the virtues of a "borderless" world and "planetary consciousness." The resulting collisions, reflecting the sharply differing needs of two radically different civilizations, could provoke some of the worst bloodshed in the years to come.

If today's redivision of the world from two into three parts seems less than obvious right now, it is simply because the transition from Second Wave brute-force economies to Third Wave brain-force economies is nowhere yet complete.

Even in the United States, Japan and Europe, the domestic battle for control between Third and Second Wave elites is still not over. Important Second Wave institutions and sectors of production still remain, and Second Wave political lobbies still cling to power.

The "mix" of Second and Third Wave elements in each high-tech country gives each its own characteristic "formation." Nevertheless, the trajectories are clear. The globally competitive race will be won by the countries that complete their Third Wave transformation with the least amount of domestic dislocation and unrest.

In the meantime, the historic change from a bisected to a trisected world could well trigger the deepest power struggles on the planet, as each country tries to position itself in the emerging three-tiered power structure. Behind this monumental reallocation of power lies a change in the role, significance and nature of knowledge.

THE ULTIMATE
SUBSTITUTE

Anyone reading this page has an amazing skill called literacy. It comes as a shock sometimes to remember that all of us had ancestors who were illiterate. Not stupid or ignorant, but invincibly illiterate.

Not only illiterate, they were also "innumerate," meaning they couldn't do the simplest arithmetic. Those few who could were deemed downright dangerous. A marvelous warning attributed to Augustine holds that Christians should stay away from people who could add or subtract. It was obvious they had "made a covenant with the Devil."

It wasn't until a thousand years later that we find "reckoning masters" teaching pupils bound for commercial careers.

What this underscores is that many of the simplest skills taken for granted in business today are the products of centuries and millennia of cumulative cultural development. Knowledge from China, from India, from the Arabs, from Phoenician traders as well as from the West, is an unrecognized part of the heritage relied on today by business executives all over the world. Successive generations have learned these skills, adapted them, transmitted them, and then slowly built on the results.

All economic systems sit upon a "knowledge base." All

business enterprises depend on the preexistence of this socially constructed resource. Unlike capital, labor and land, it is usually neglected by economists and business executives when calculating the inputs needed for production. Yet this resource is now the most important of all.

Today we are living through one of those exclamation points in history when the entire structure of human knowledge is once again trembling with change as old barriers fall. We are not just accumulating more facts. Just as we are now restructuring companies and whole economies, we are totally reorganizing the production and distribution of knowledge and the symbols used to communicate it.

What does this mean? It means that we are creating new networks of knowledge . . . linking concepts to one another in startling ways . . . building up amazing hierarchies of inference . . . spawning new theories, hypotheses and images based on novel assumptions, new languages, codes and logics. Businesses, governments and individuals are collecting and storing more sheer data than any previous generation in history.

But more important, we are interrelating data in more ways, giving them context and thus forming them into information; and we are assembling chunks of in formation into larger and larger models and architectures of knowledge.

Not all this new knowledge is "correct," factual, or even explicit. Much knowledge, as the term is used here, is unspoken, consisting of assumptions piled atop assumptions, of fragmentary models, of unnoticed analogies, and it includes not simply logical and seemingly unemotional information or data, but values, the products of passion and emotion, not to mention imagination and intuition.

It is today's gigantic upheaval in the knowledge base of society—not computer hype or mere financial manipulation— that explains the rise of a super- symbolic, Third Wave economy.

Many changes in the society's knowledge system translate directly into business operations. This *knowledge system* is an even more pervasive part of every firm's environment than the banking system, the political system, or the energy system.

Apart from the fact that no business could open its doors if there were no language, culture, data, information and know-how, there is the deeper fact that of all the resources needed to create wealth, none is more versatile than knowledge.

Take Second Wave mass production. In most smokestack factories it was inordinately expensive to change any product. It required highly paid tool-and- die makers, jig setters and other specialists, it and resulted in extended downtime during which the machines were idle and ate up capital, interest and overhead. That's why cost per unit went down if you could make longer and longer runs of identical products. This gave rise to the theory of economies of scale.

But the new technology stands Second Wave theories on their heads. Instead of mass production, we are moving towards de-massified production. The result is an explosion of customized and semicustomized products and services. The latest computer-driven manufacturing technologies make endless variety possible and inexpensive.

New information technologies, in fact, push the cost of diversity toward zero and reduce the once vital economies of scale.

Or take materials. A smart computer program hitched to a lathe can cut more pieces out of the same amount of steel than most human operators. Making miniaturization possible, new knowledge leads to smaller, lighter products, which, in turn, cuts down on warehousing and transportation. Up-to-the-minute tracking of shipments—i.e., better information—means further transportation savings.

New knowledge also leads to the creation of totally new materials ranging from aircraft composites to biologicals and increases our ability to substitute one material for another. Deeper knowledge now permits us to customize materials at the molecular level to produce desired thermal, electrical or mechanical characteristics.

The only reason we ship huge amounts of raw materials like bauxite or nickel or copper across the planet is that we lack the knowledge to convert local materials into usable substitutes. Once we acquire that know-how, further drastic savings in transportation will result. In short, knowledge is a substitute for both resources and shipping.

The same goes for energy. Nothing illustrates the substitutability of knowledge for other resources better than the recent breakthroughs in superconductivity, which at a minimum will drive down the amount of energy that now must be transmitted for each unit of output.

In addition to substituting for materials, transportation and energy, knowledge also saves time. Time itself is one of the most important of economic resources, even though it shows up nowhere on a Second Wave company's balance sheet. Time remains, in effect, a hidden input. Especially when change accelerates, the ability to shorten time—for instance, by communicating swiftly or by bringing new products to market fast—can be the difference between profit and loss.

New knowledge speeds things up, drives us toward a real-time, instantaneous economy, and substitutes for time.

Space, too, is conserved and conquered by knowledge. GE's Transportation Systems division builds locomotives. When it began using advanced in formation processing and communications to link up with its suppliers, it was able to turn over its inventory twelve times faster than before and to save a full acre of warehouse space.

Not only miniaturized products and reduced warehousing but other savings are possible. Advanced information technologies, including document scanning and new telecommunications capacity based on computers and advanced knowledge, make it possible to disperse production out of high-cost urban centers and to reduce energy and transport costs even further.

KNOWLEDGE VERSUS CAPITAL

So much is written about the substitution of computerized equipment for human labor that we often ignore the ways in which it also substitutes for capital.

Indeed, in a sense knowledge is a far greater long-term threat to the power of finance than are organized labor or anticapitalist political parties. For, relatively speaking, the information revolution is reducing the need for capital per unit of output in a capitalist economy. Nothing could be more revolutionary.

Vittorio Merloni is a sixty-one-year-old Italian businessman. Ten percent of all the washing machines, refrigerators and other major household appliances sold in Europe are made by Merloni's company. His main competitors are Electrolux of Sweden and Philips of Holland.

According to Merloni, "we need less capital now to do the same thing" that required more capital in the past. "This means that a poor country can be much better off today with the same amount of capital than five or ten years ago."

The reason, he says, is that knowledge-based technologies are reducing the capital needed to produce dishwashers, stoves or vacuum cleaners.

To begin with, information substitutes for high-cost inventory, according to Merloni. By speeding the responsiveness of the factory to the market and making short runs economical, better and more instantaneous information makes it possible to reduce the amount of components and finished goods sitting in warehouses or railroad sidings. Merloni at one point cut a startling sixty percent from his inventory costs.

Merloni's case has been duplicated by every major company in the United States, Japan and Germany as just-in-time delivery of parts, based on computerized information, is slashing inventories everywhere.

Cuts in inventory, of course, not only translate back into the smaller space and real estate costs mentioned earlier, but also into reduced taxes, insurance and overhead.

Even though the initial cost of computers, software, information and telecommunications may itself be high, Merloni says the overall savings mean that his company needs less capital to do the same job it did in the past.

Michael Milken, who for better or worse knows a thing or two about investment, has summed it up in six words: "Human capital has replaced dollar capital."

Because it reduces the need for raw materials, labor, time, space, capital and other inputs, knowledge becomes the ultimate substitute—the central resource of an advanced economy. And as this happens, its value soars.

THE WAY WE MAKE WEALTH

In 1956 the Soviet Union's strongman, Nikita Khrushchev, uttered his famous boast—"We will bury you." What he meant was that communism would outstrip capitalism economically in the years ahead. The boast carried with it as well the threat of military defeat, and it reverberated around the world.

Yet few at the time even dimly suspected just how a revolution in the West's system for creating wealth would transform the world military balance—and the nature of warfare itself.

What Khrushchev (and most Americans) didn't know was that 1956 was also the first year in which white-collar and service employees outnumbered blue- collar factory workers in the United States—an early indication that the Second Wave's smokestack economy was fading and a new, Third Wave economy was being born.

To understand the extraordinary changes that have since occurred and to anticipate the even more dramatic changes that lie ahead, we need to look at the main features of the new Third Wave economy. Here, then, at the risk of minor repetition, are the keys not only to business profitability and global competitiveness but to the political economy of the twenty-first century.

41

1. FACTORS OF PRODUCTION

While land, labor, raw materials and capital were the main factors of production in the Second Wave economy of the past, knowledge—broadly defined here to include data, information, images, symbols, culture, ideology and values—is now the central resource of the Third Wave economy.

As we have seen, the appropriate data, information and/or knowledge make it possible to reduce all the other inputs used to create wealth. But the concept of knowledge as the "ultimate substitute" is still not widely grasped. Most economists and accountants are mystified and put off by this idea because it is hard to quantify.

What makes the Third Wave economy revolutionary is the fact that while land, labor, raw materials and perhaps even capital can be regarded as finite resources, knowledge is for all intents inexhaustible. Unlike a single blast furnace or assembly line, knowledge can be used by two companies at the same time. And they can use it to generate still more knowledge. Thus, Second Wave economic theories based on finite, exhaustible inputs are inapplicable to Third Wave economies.

2. INTANGIBLE VALUES

While the value of a Second Wave company might be measured in terms of its hard assets like buildings, machines, stocks and inventory, the value of successful Third Wave firms increasingly lies in their capacity for acquiring, generating, distributing and applying knowledge strategically and operationally.

The real value of companies like Compaq or Kodak, Hitachi or Siemens, depends more on the ideas, insights and information in the heads of their employees and in the data banks and patents these companies control than on the trucks, assembly lines and other physical assets they may have. Thus capital itself is now increasingly based on intangibles.

3. DE-MASSIFICATION

Mass production, the defining characteristic of the Second Wave economy, becomes increasingly obsolete as firms install information intensive, often robotized manufacturing systems capable of endless cheap variation, even customization. The revolutionary result is, in effect, the de-massification of mass production.

The shift toward smart flex-techs promotes diversity and feeds consumer choice to the point that a Wal-Mart store can offer the buyer nearly 110,000 products in various types, sizes, models and colors to choose among.

But Wal-Mart is a mass merchandiser. Increasingly, the mass market itself is breaking up into differentiated niches as customer needs diverge and better information makes it possible for businesses to identify and serve micro-markets. Specialty stores, boutiques, superstores, TV home-shopping systems, computer- based buying, direct mail and other systems provide a growing diversity of channels through which producers can distribute their wares to customers in an increasingly de-massified marketplace. When we wrote *Future Shock* in the late 1960s, visionary marketers began talking about "market segmentation." Today they no longer focus on "segments" but on "particles"—family units and even single individuals.

Meanwhile, advertising is targeted at smaller and smaller market segments reached through increasingly de-massified media. The dramatic breakup of mass audiences is underscored by the crisis of the once great TV networks, ABC, CBS and NBC, at a time when Tele-Communications, Inc. of Denver, announces a fiber-optic network capable of providing viewers with five hundred interactive channels of television. Such systems mean that sellers will be able to target buyers with even greater precision. The simultaneous de-massification of production, distribution and communication revolutionizes the economy and shifts it from homogeneity to ward extreme heterogeneity.

4. WORK

Work itself is transformed. Low-skilled, essentially interchangeable muscle work drove the Second Wave. Mass, factory-style education prepared workers for routine, repetitive labor. By contrast, the Third Wave is accompanied by a growing non-interchangeability of labor as skill requirements skyrocket.

Muscle power is essentially fungible. Thus a low-skilled worker who quits or is fired can be replaced quickly and with little cost. By contrast, the rising levels of specialized skills required in the Third Wave economy make finding the right person with the right skills harder and more costly.

Although he or she may face competition from many other jobless muscle workers, a janitor laid off from a giant defense firm can take a janitor's job in a school or an insurance office. By contrast, the electronics engineer who has spent years building satellites does not necessarily have the skills needed by a firm doing environmental engineering. A gynecologist can't do brain surgery. Rising specialization and rapid changes in skill requirements reduce the interchangeability of labor.

As economies advance, a further change is seen in the ratio of "direct" labor to "indirect" labor. In traditional terms direct or "productive" workers are those on the factory floor who actually make the product. They produce added value, and everyone else is described as "nonproductive" or making only an "indirect" contribution.

Today these distinctions blur as the ratio of factory production workers to white-collar, technical and professional workers declines even on the factory floor. At least as much value is produced by "indirect" as by "direct" labor—if not more.

5. INNOVATION

With the economies of Japan and Europe recovered from World War II, American firms face heavy competitive fire. Constant innovation is needed to compete—new ideas for products, technologies, processes, marketing, finance. Something on the order of 1,000 new products are introduced into America's supermarkets every month. Even before the model 486 computer replaced the model 386 computer, the new 586 chip was on its way. Thus smart firms encourage workers to take initiative, come up with new ideas and, even if necessary, to "throw away the rulebook."

6. SCALE

Work units shrink. The scale of operations is miniaturized along with many of the products. Vast numbers of workers doing much the same muscle work are replaced by small, differentiated work teams. Big businesses are getting smaller; small businesses are multiplying. IBM with 370,000 employees is being pecked to death by small manufacturers around the world. To survive, it lays off many workers and splits itself into thirteen different—smaller—business units.

In the Third Wave system, economies of scale are frequently outweighed by diseconomies of complexity. The more complicated the firm, the more the left hand can't anticipate what the right hand will do next. Things fall through the cracks. Problems proliferate that may outweigh any of the presumed benefits of sheer mass. The old idea that bigger is necessarily better is increasingly outmoded.

45

7. ORGANIZATION

Struggling to adapt to high-speed changes, companies are racing to dismantle their bureaucratic Second Wave structures. Industrial-era companies typically had similar tables of organization—pyramidal, monolithic and bureaucratic. Today's markets, technologies and consumer needs change so rapidly and put such varied pressures on the firm, that bureaucratic uniformity is on its way out. The search is on for wholly new forms of organization. "Re-engineering," for example, the current buzzword in management, seeks to restructure the firm around processes rather than markets or compartmentalized specialties.

Relatively standardized structures give way to matrix organizations, "ad hocratic" project teams, profit centers, as well as to a growing diversity of strategic alliances, joint ventures and consortia—many of these crossing national boundaries. Since markets change constantly, position is less important than flexibility and maneuverability.

8. SYSTEMS INTEGRATION

Rising complexity in the economy calls for more sophisticated integration and management. In a not atypical case Nabisco, the food company, has to fill 500 orders a day for literally hundreds of thousands of different products that must be shipped from 49 factories and 13 distribution centers, and at the same time take into account 30,000 different sales promotional deals with its customers.

Managing such complexity requires new forms of leadership and an extremely high order of systemic integration. That, in turn, requires greater and greater volumes of information to pulse through the organization.

9. INFRASTRUCTURE

To hold everything together—to track all the components and products, to synchronize deliveries, to keep engineers and marketers apprised of each other's plans, to alert the R&D people to the needs of the manufacturing side and, above all, to give management a coherent picture of what is going on—billions of dollars are being poured into electronic networks that link computers, data bases and other information technologies together.

This vast electronic information structure, frequently satellite based, knits whole companies together, often linking them into the computers and networks of suppliers and customers as well. Other networks link networks. Japan has targeted $250 billion to develop better, faster networks over the next twenty-five years. The White House now is promoting its controversial plan for an "information superhighway." Whatever we may think of the plan or the metaphor, one thing is clear: electronic pathways form the essential infrastructure of the Third Wave economy.

10. ACCELERATION

All these changes further accelerate the pace of operations and transactions. Economies of speed replace economies of scale. Competition is so intense and the speeds required so high that the old "time is money" rule is increasingly updated to "every interval of time is worth more than the one before it."

Time becomes a critical variable as reflected in "just-in-time" deliveries and a pressure to reduce DIP or "decisions in process." Slow, sequential, step-by-step engineering is replaced by "simultaneous engineering." Companies wage "time-based competition." Expressing the new urgency, DuWayne Peterson, a top executive at Merrill Lynch, says, "Money moves at the speed of light. Information has to move faster." Thus acceleration pushes Third Wave business closer and closer to real time.

(47)

* * * *

Taken together, these ten features of the Third Wave economy, among many others, add up to a monumental change in how wealth is created. The conversion of the United States, Japan and Europe to this new system, though not yet complete, represents the single most important change in the global economy since the spread of factories brought about by the industrial revolution.

This historical transformation, picking up speed in the early- to mid-1970s, was already fairly well advanced by the 1990s. Unfortunately, much of America's economic thinking was left behind.

FIVE

MATERIAL-ISMO!

One day, while Ronald Reagan was still in the White House, a small group assembled around the table in the Family Dining Room to discuss the long-range future of America. The group consisted of eight well-known futurists, and was joined by the Vice President and three of Reagan's top advisers, among them Donald Regan, the President's newly appointed chief of staff.

The meeting had been convened by the authors at the request of the White House and opened with the statement that, while futurists differed on many technological, social and political issues, there was common agreement that the economy was going through a deep transformation.

The words were hardly voiced when Donald Regan snapped, "So you all think we're going to go around cutting each other's hair and flipping hamburgers! Aren't we going to be a great manufacturing power anymore?"

The President and Vice President looked around expectantly for a reply. Most of the men at the table seemed taken aback by the brusqueness and immediacy of his attack. It was Heidi Toffler who answered. "No Mr. Regan," she replied patiently, "the United States will continue to be a great manufacturing power. There just won't be as high a percentage of people working in factories."

Explaining the difference between traditional manufacturing methods and the way Macintosh computers were then being produced, she pointed out that the United States was surely one of the great food producers in the world with fewer than two percent of the work force engaged in agriculture. In fact, throughout the past century the more its farm labor force shrank relative to other sectors, the stronger, not weaker, the United States became as an agricultural power. Why couldn't the same be true of manufacture?

The startling fact remains that after many ups and downs, manufacturing employment in the United States in 1988 was almost exactly the same as it was in 1968: slightly over nineteen million. Manufacturing contributed the same percentage of national output as it did thirty years earlier. But it was doing all this with a smaller fraction of the total work force.

Moreover, the handwriting is clear: because American population and the labor force are both likely to expand and because many American manufacturers have automated and reorganized in the 1980s and 1990s, the shrinkage of factory employment relative to the total must continue. While the United States, according to some estimates, is likely to generate 10,000 new jobs a day for the next decade, few if any will be in the manufacturing sector. A similar process has been transforming the European and Japanese economies as well.

Nevertheless, even now Donald Regan's words are still occasionally echoed by captains of badly run American industries, union leaders with dwindling membership rolls and economists or historians who beat the drum for the importance of manufacturing—as though anyone had suggested the reverse.

Behind much of this rhetoric is the notion that the shift of employment from manual work to service and mental-sector jobs is somehow bad for the economy and that a small manufacturing sector (in terms of jobs) leaves the economy "hollowed out."

Such arguments recall the views of the French *physiocrats* of the eighteenth-century who, unable to imagine an industrial economy, regarded agriculture as the only "productive" activity.

THE NEW MEANING OF JOBLESSNESS

Much of the lamentation over the "decline" of manufacture is fed by Second Wave self-interest and based on obsolete concepts of wealth, production and unemployment.

Since the 1960s, the shift away from Second Wave manual labor toward Third Wave service work and super-symbolic activity has become widespread, dramatic and irreversible. In the United States today these activities account for fully three-quarters of the work force. The great transition is reflected globally in the surprising fact that world exports of services and "intellectual property" are now equal to those of electronics and autos combined, or of the combined exports in food and fuels.

The authors and other futurists foreshadowed this massive shift as early as the 1960s. But because the early warnings were ignored, the transition has been unnecessarily rocky. Mass layoffs, bankruptcies and other upheavals swept through the economy as old rust-belt industries, late to install computers, robots and electronic information systems and slow to restructure, found themselves gutted by more fleet-footed competition. Many blamed their troubles on foreign competition, high or low interest rates, overregulation and a thousand other factors.

Some of these no doubt played a role. But equally to blame was the arrogance of the most powerful smokestack companies— auto makers, steel mills, shipyards, textile firms—that had for so long dominated the economy. Their managerial myopia punished those in the society least responsible for industrial backwardness and least able to protect themselves—their workers.

The fact that aggregate manufacturing employment in 1988

was at the same level as 1968 doesn't mean that the workers laid off in between simply returned to their old jobs. On the contrary, with more Third Wave technologies in place, companies needed a radically different kind of work force as well.

The old Second Wave factories needed essentially interchangeable workers. By contrast, Third Wave operations require diverse and continually evolving skills—which means that workers become less and less interchangeable. And this turns the entire problem of unemployment upside down.

In Second Wave or smokestack societies an injection of capital spending or consumer purchasing power could stimulate the economy and generate jobs. Given one million jobless, one could, in principle, prime the economy and create one million jobs. Since the jobs were either interchangeable or required so little skill that they could be learned in less than an hour, virtually any unemployed worker could fill almost any job.

In today's super-symbolic economy this is less true—which is why a lot of unemployment seems intractable, and neither the traditional Keynesian nor monetarist remedies work well. To cope with the Great Depression, John Maynard Keynes, we recall, urged deficit spending by government to put money into consumers' pockets. Once consumers had the money, they would rush out and buy things. This in turn would lead manufacturers to expand their plants and hire more workers. Good-bye, unemployment. Monetarists urged manipulation of interest rates or money supply instead, to increase or decrease purchasing power as needed.

In today's global economy, pumping money into the consumer's pocket may simply send it flowing overseas without doing anything to help the domestic economy. An American buying a new TV set or compact disc player merely sends dollars to Japan, Korea, Malaysia or elsewhere. The purchase doesn't add jobs at home.

But there is a far more basic flaw in the old strategies: they still focus on the circulation of money rather than knowledge. Yet it is no longer possible to reduce joblessness simply by increasing the number of jobs because the problem is no longer merely numbers. Unemployment has gone from quantitative to qualitative.

The jobless desperately need money if they and their families are to survive, and it is both necessary and morally right to provide them with decent levels of public assistance. But any effective strategy for reducing joblessness in a super-symbolic economy must depend less on the allocation of wealth and more on the allocation of knowledge.

Furthermore, as these new jobs are not likely to be found in what we still think of as manufacture, we will need to prepare people through schooling, apprenticeships and on-the-job learning for work in such fields as the human services—helping to care, for example, for our fast-growing population of the elderly, providing child care, health services, personal security, training services, leisure and recreation services, tourism and the like.

We will also have to begin according human- service jobs the same respect previously reserved for manufacture rather than snidely denigrating the entire service sector as "hamburger flipping." McDonald's cannot stand as the sole symbol for a range of activities that includes everything from teaching to working at a dating service or in a hospital radiology center.

What's more, if, as is often charged, wages are low in the service sector, then the solution is to increase service productivity and to invent new forms of work-force organization and collective bargaining. Unions, primarily designed for the crafts or for mass manufacturing, need to be totally transformed or else replaced by new-style organizations more appropriate to the super-symbolic economy. To survive they will have to support rather than resist such things as work-at-home programs, flextime and job-sharing.

In brief, the rise of the super-symbolic economy compels us to reconceptualize the entire problem of unemployment from the ground up. To challenge outworn assumptions, however, is also to challenge those who benefit from them. The Third Wave system of wealth creation thus threatens long-entrenched power relationships in corporations, unions and governments.

THE SPECTRUM OF MIND WORK

The super-symbolic economy makes obsolete not only our concepts of unemployment but our concepts of work as well. To understand it and the power struggles that it triggers, we will even need a fresh vocabulary.

Thus, even the division of the economy into such sectors as "agriculture," "manufacturing" and "services" today obscures, rather than clarifies. Today's high-speed changes blur once-neat distinctions. Instead of clinging to the old classifications, we need to look behind the labels and ask what people in these companies actually do to create added value. Once we pose this question, we find that more and more of the work in all three sectors consists of symbolic processing, or "mind work."

Farmers now use computers to calculate grain feeds; steelworkers monitor consoles and video screens; investment bankers switch on their laptops as they model financial markets. It matters little whether economists choose to label these as "agricultural," "manufacturing" or "service" activities.

Even occupational categories are breaking down. To label someone a stockroom attendant, a machine operator, or a sales representative conceals rather than reveals. It is a lot more useful today to group workers by the amount of symbolic processing or mind work they do as part of their jobs regardless of the label they wear or whether they happen to work in a store, a truck, a factory, a hospital or an office.

In what might be called the "mind-work spectrum" we have the research scientist, the financial analyst, the computer programmer or, for that matter, the ordinary file clerk. Why include file clerks and scientists in the same group? The answer is that, while their functions obviously differ and they work at vastly different levels of abstraction, both—and millions like them—do nothing but move information around or generate more information. Their work is totally symbolic.

In the middle of the mind-work spectrum we find a broad range of "mixed" jobs—tasks requiring the worker to perform physical labor but also handle information. The Federal Express or United Parcel Service driver also operates a computer at his or her side. In advanced factories the machine operator is a highly trained information worker. The hotel clerk, the nurse, and many others have to deal with people—but spend a considerable fraction of their time generating, getting or giving out information.

Auto mechanics at Ford dealers, for example, may still have greasy hands, but they also use a computer system designed by Hewlett-Packard that provides them with an "expert system" to help them in trouble-shooting along with instant access to one hundred megabytes of technical drawings and data stored on CD-ROM. The system asks them for data about the car they are fixing; it permits them to search through the masses of technical material intuitively; it makes inferences and then guides them through the repair steps.

When they are interacting with this system, are they "mechanics" or "mind workers"?

It is the purely manual jobs at the bottom end of the spectrum that are disappearing. With fewer manual jobs in the economy, the "proletariat" is now a minority, replaced increasingly by a "cognitariat." More accurately, as the super-symbolic economy unfolds, the proletariat _becomes_ a cognitariat.

The key questions about a person's work today have to do with how much of the job entails information processing, how routine or programmable it is, what level of abstractions is involved, what access the person has to the central data bank and management information system and how much autonomy and responsibility the individual enjoys.

LOWBROWS VERSUS HIGHBROWS

Such immense changes cannot come without power conflict, and to anticipate who will gain and who will lose, it may help to think of companies on a similar mind-work spectrum.

We need to classify companies not by whether they are nominally in manufacturing or services but by what their people actually do.

CSX, for example, is a firm that operates railroads throughout the eastern half of the United States along with one of the world's biggest oceangoing containerization businesses. But CSX increasingly sees itself as being in the information business.

Says Alex Mandl of CSX: "The information component of our service package is growing bigger and bigger. It's not just enough to deliver products. Customers want information. Where their products will be consolidated and de-consolidated, what time each item will be where, prices, customs information and much more. We are an information-driven business." Which means that the proportion of CSX employees in the middle and higher ranges of the mind-work spectrum is increasing.

What this suggests is that companies can be roughly classified as "highbrow," "middlebrow" or "lowbrow," depending on how knowledge-intensive they are. Some firms and industries need to process more information than others in order to produce wealth. Like individual jobs, they can be positioned on the mind-work spectrum according to the amount and complexity of the mind work they do.

Lowbrow firms typically concentrate mind work in a few people at the top, leaving muscle work or mindless work to everyone else. Their operating assumption is that workers are ignorant or that, in any case, their knowledge is irrelevant to production.

Even in the highbrow sector today one may find examples of "de-skilling"—simplifying jobs, reducing them to their smallest components, monitoring output stroke by stroke. These attempts to apply methods de signed by Frederick Taylor for use in factories at the beginning of the twentieth century are, however, the wave of the lowbrow past, not the highbrow future. For any task that is so repetitive and simple that it can be done without thought is, eventually, a candidate for robotization.

As the economy moves more toward Third Wave production, all firms are being compelled to rethink the role of knowledge. The smartest firms in the highbrow sector are the first to rethink the role of knowledge and to redesign work itself. They operate on the assumption that productivity and profits will both skyrocket if mindless work is reduced to a minimum or transferred to advanced technology and the full potential of the worker is tapped. The goal is a better paid but smaller, smarter work force.

Even middlebrow operations that still require physical manipulation of things are becoming more knowledge-intensive, moving up the mind-work spectrum.

Highbrow firms, in general, are not charitable institutions. Although the work in them tends to be less physically onerous than in lowbrow operations and the surroundings more agreeable, these firms typically demand *more* of their employees than lowbrow firms do. Employees are encouraged to use not only their rational minds but to pour their emotions, intuitions and imagination into the job. This is why Marcusian critics see in this an even more sinister "exploitation" of the employee.

(57)

LOWBROW IDEOLOGY

In lowbrow industrial economies, wealth was typically measured by the possession of goods. The production of goods was regarded as central to the economy. Conversely, symbolic and service activities, while unavoidable, were stigmatized as nonproductive. The manufacture of goods—autos, radios, tractors, TV sets—was seen as "male" or *macho* and words like *practical, realistic* or *hardheaded* were associated with it. By contrast, the production of knowledge or the exchange of information was typically disparaged as mere "paper pushing."

A flood of corollaries flowed from these attitudes. For example, that "production" is the combination of material resources, machines and muscle . . . that the most important assets of a firm are tangibles . . . that national wealth flows from a surplus of the trade in goods . . . that trade in services is significant only because it facilitates trade in goods . . . that most education is a waste unless it is narrowly vocational . . . that research is airy-fairy . . . and that the liberal arts are irrelevant or, worse yet, inimical to business success. What mattered, in short, was matter.

Ideas like these were by no means limited to the Babbitts of capitalism. They had their analogs in the communist world as well. Marxist economists, if any thing, have had a harder time trying to integrate high brow work into their schema, and "socialist realism" in the arts produced thousands of portrayals of happy workers, their Schwarzenegger-like muscles straining against a background of cogwheels, smokestacks and steam locomotives. The glorification of the proletariat and the theory that it was the vanguard of change, reflected the principles of a lowbrow economy.

What all this added up to was more than a welter of isolated opinions, assumptions and attitudes. Rather it formed a self-reinforcing, self-justifying ideology based on a kind of macho materialism—a brash, triumphant "material-ismo!" Material-ismo, in fact, was the ideology of Second Wave mass manufacture.

There was a time when material-ismo may have made sense. Today, when the real value of most products lies in the knowledge embedded in them, it is both reactionary and imbecile. Any country that chooses to pursue policies based on material-ismo condemns itself to becoming the Bangladesh of the twenty-first century.

HIGHBROW IDEOLOGY

The companies, institutions and people with a strong stake in the Third Wave economy haven't yet fashioned a coherent counter-rationale. But some of the underlying ideas are falling into place.

The first fragmentary foundations of this new economics can be glimpsed in the still-unrecognized writings of people like the late Eugene Loebl who, during eleven years in a communist prison in Czechoslovakia, deeply rethought the assumptions of both Marxist and Western economics; Henry K. H. Woo of Hong Kong, who has analyzed "the unseen dimensions of wealth;" Orio Giarini in Geneva, who applies the concepts of risk and indeterminacy in his analysis of services of the future; and the American Walter Weisskopf, who writes on the role of non-equilibrium conditions in economic development.

Scientists today are asking how systems behave in turbulence, how order evolves out of chaotic conditions and how developing systems leap to higher levels of diversity. Such questions are extremely pertinent to business and the economy. Management books speak of "thriving on chaos." Economists rediscover the work of Joseph Schumpeter, who spoke of "creative destruction" as necessary to advance. In a storm of takeovers, divestitures, reorganizations, bankruptcies, start-ups, joint ventures and internal reorganizations, the entire economy is taking on a new structure that is light-years more diverse, fast-changing and complex than the old smokestack economy.

This "leap" to a higher level of diversity, speed and complexity requires a corresponding leap to higher, more sophisticated forms of integration. In turn, this demands radically higher levels of knowledge processing.

Drawing heavily on the seventeenth-century writings of René Descartes, the culture of industrialism rewarded people who could break problems and processes down into smaller and smaller constituent parts. This disintegrative or analytic approach, when transferred to economics, led us to think of production as a series of disconnected steps.

The new model of production that springs from the super-symbolic economy is dramatically different. Based on a systemic or integrative view, it sees production as increasingly simultaneous and synthesized. The parts of the process are not the whole, and they cannot be isolated from one another.

We are in fact discovering that "production" neither begins nor ends in the factory. Thus, the latest models of economic production extend the process both upstream and downstream—forward into aftercare or "support" for the product even after it is sold, as in auto-repair warrantees or the support expected from the retailer when a person buys a computer. Before long the conception of production will reach even beyond that to ecologically safe disposal of the product after use. Companies will have to provide for post-use cleanup, forcing them to alter design specs, cost calculations, production methods and much else besides. In so doing they will be performing more service relative to manufacture, and they will be adding value. "Production" will be seen to include all these functions.

Similarly, they may extend the definition backward to include such functions as training of the employee, provision of day care and other services. An unhappy muscle-worker could be compelled to be "productive." In high-symbolic activities, happy workers produce more. Hence, productivity begins even before the worker arrives at the office. To old-timers, such an expanded definition of production may seem fuzzy or nonsensical. To the new generation of super-symbolic leaders, conditioned to think systematically rather than in terms of isolated steps, it will seem natural.

In brief, production is reconceptualized as a far more encompassing process than the economists and ideologists of lowbrow economics imagined. And at every step from today on, it is knowledge, not cheap labor, and symbols, not raw materials, that embody and add value.

This deep reconceptualization of the sources of added value is fraught with consequence. It smashes the assumptions of both free-marketism and Marxism alike, and the material-ismo that gave rise to both. Thus, the ideas that value is sweated from the back of the worker alone and that value is produced by the glorious capitalist entrepreneur, both implied in material-ismo, are revealed to be false and misleading politically as well as economically.

In the new economy the receptionist and the investment banker who assembles the capital, the key punch operator and the salesperson, as well as the systems designer and telecommunications specialist all add value. Even more significantly, so does the customer. Value results from a total effort rather than from one isolated step in the process.

The rising importance of mind-work will not go away, no matter how many scare stories are published warning about the dire consequences of a "vanishing" manufacturing base or deriding the concept of the "information economy." Neither will the new conception of how wealth is created.

For what we are watching is a mighty convergence of Third Wave changes—the transformation of production coming together with the transformation of capital and money itself. Together they form a revolutionary new system for wealth creation on the planet.

61

SIX

SOCIALISM'S COLLISION WITH THE FUTURE

The dramatic death of state socialism in Eastern Europe and its bloody anguish from Bucharest to Baku to Beijing did not happen by accident. Socialism collided with the future. Socialist regimes did not collapse because of CIA plots, capitalist encirclement or economic strangulation from outside. Eastern European communist governments toppled domino-fashion as soon as Moscow sent the message that it would no longer use troops to protect them from their own people. But the crisis of socialism as a system in the Soviet Union, China and elsewhere was far more deeply based.

Just as Gutenberg's invention of movable type in the mid-fifteenth century ignited the Protestant Reformation—so the appearance of the computer and new communications media in the mid-twentieth century smashed Moscow's control of the mind in the countries it ruled or held captive.

Mind workers were typically dismissed as "nonproductive" by Marxist economists (and many classical economists as well). Yet it is these supposedly nonproductive workers who, perhaps more than any other, have given Western economies a tremendous shot of adrenaline since the mid-fifties.

Today, even with all their supposed "contradictions" unresolved, the high-tech capitalist nations have swept far ahead

ALVIN AND HEIDI TOFFLER

of the rest of the world in economic terms. It was computer-based capitalism, not smokestack socialism, that made what Marxists call a "qualitative leap" forward. With the real revolution spreading in the high-tech nations, the socialist nations had become, in effect, a deeply reactionary bloc led by elderly men imbued with a nineteenth-century theology. Mikhail Gorbachev was the first Soviet leader to recognize this historic fact.

In a 1989 speech, some thirty years after the new system of wealth creation began to appear in the United States, Gorbachev declared, "We were nearly one of the last to realize that in the age of information science the most expensive asset is knowledge."

Marx himself had given the classic definition of a revolutionary moment. It came, he said, when the "social relations of production" (meaning the nature of ownership and control) prevent further development of the "means of production" (roughly speaking, the technology).

That formula perfectly described the socialist world crisis. Just as feudal "social relations" once hindered industrial development, now socialist "social relations" made it all but impossible for socialist countries to take advantage of the new wealth-creation system based on computers, communication and, above all, on open information. In fact, the central failure of the great state socialist experiment of the twentieth century lay in its obsolete ideas about knowledge.

THE PRE-CYBERNETIC MACHINE

With minor exceptions, state socialism led not to affluence, equality and freedom, but to a one-party political system, a massive bureaucracy, heavy-handed secret police, government control of the media, secrecy and the repression of intellectual and artistic freedom.

Setting aside the oceans of spurting blood needed to prop it up, a close look at this system reveals that every one of these elements is not just a way of organizing people but also—and more profoundly—a particular way of organizing, channeling and controlling knowledge.

A one-party political system is designed to control political communication. Since no other party exists, it restricts the diversity of political information flowing through the society, blocking feedback and thus blinding those in power to the full complexity of their problems. With very narrowly defined information flowing upward through the approved channel and commands flowing downward, it becomes very difficult for the system to detect errors and correct them.

In fact, top-down control in the socialist countries was based increasingly on lies and misinformation since reporting bad news up the line was often risky. The decision to run a one-party system is a decision, above all, about knowledge.

The overpowering bureaucracy that socialism created in every sphere of life was also a knowledge-restricting device, forcing knowledge into pre-defined compartments or cubbyholes and restricting communication to "official channels," while de-legitimating informal communication and organization.

The secret police apparatus, state control of the media, the intimidation of intellectuals and the repression of artistic freedom all represent further attempts to limit and control information flows.

In fact, behind each of these elements we find a single obsolete assumption about knowledge: the arrogant belief that those in command—whether of the party or of the state—should decide what others should know.

These features of all the state socialist nations guaranteed economic stupidity and derived from the concept of the pre-cybernetic machine as applied to society and life itself. Second Wave machines for the most part operated without any feedback. Plug in the power, start the motor, and they run irrespective of what is happening in the outside environment.

Third Wave machines, by contrast, are intelligent. They have sensors that suck in information from the environment, detect changes and adapt the operation of the machine accordingly. They are self-regulating. The technological difference is revolutionary.

But Marxist theoreticians remained stuck in the Second Wave past, as even their language suggests. Thus for Marxian socialists the class struggle was the "locomotive of history." A key task was to capture the "state machine." And society itself, being machine-like, could be preset to deliver abundance and freedom. Lenin, on capturing control of Russia in 1917, became the supreme mechanic.

A brilliant intellectual, Lenin understood the importance of ideas. But, for him, symbolic production—the mind itself—could be programmed. Marx wrote of freedom, but Lenin, on taking power, undertook to engineer knowledge. Thus he insisted that all art, culture, science, journalism and symbolic activity in general be placed at the service of a master plan for society. In time each branch of learning would be neatly organized into an "academy" with fixed bureaucratic departments and ranks all subject to party and state control. "Cultural workers" would be employed by institutions controlled by a Ministry of Culture. Publishing and broadcasting would be monopolies of the state. Knowledge, in effect, would be made part of the state machine.

This constipated approach to knowledge blocked economic development even in low-level, smokestack economies; it is diametrically opposed to the principles needed for economic advancement in the age of the computer.

THE PROPERTY PARADOX

The Third Wave wealth-creation system now spreading also challenges three pillars of the socialist faith. Take the question of property.

From the beginning, socialists traced poverty, depressions, unemployment and the other evils of industrialism to private ownership of the means of production. The way to solve these ills was for the workers to own the factories—through the state or through collectives.

Once this was accomplished, things would be different. No more competitive waste. Completely rational planning. Production for use rather than profit. Intelligent investment to drive the economy forward. The dream of abundance for all would be realized for the first time in history.

In the nineteenth century when these ideas were formulated, they seemed to reflect the most advanced scientific knowledge of the time. Marxists, in fact, claimed to have gone beyond fuzzy-headed utopianism and arrived at truly "scientific socialism." Utopians might dream of self-governing communal villages. Scientific socialists knew that in a developing smokestack society such notions were impractical. Utopians like Charles Fourier looked toward the agrarian past. Scientific socialists looked toward what was then the industrial future.

Thus, later on, while socialist regimes experimented with cooperatives, worker-management, communes and other schemes, state ownership became the dominant form of property throughout the socialist world. Everywhere the state, not the workers, thus became the chief beneficiary of socialist revolution.

Socialism failed to meet its promise to improve radically the material conditions of life. When living standards fell in the Soviet Union after the revolution, the decline was blamed, with some justification, on the effects of World War I and counterrevolution. Later the shortfalls were blamed on capitalist encirclement. Still later, on World War II. Yet forty years after the war, staples like coffee and oranges were still in short supply in Moscow.

Remarkably, though their number is declining, one still hears orthodox socialists around the world calling for the nationalization of industry and finance. From Brazil and Peru to South Africa and, even in the industrialized nations of the West, there remain true believers who, despite all historical evidence to the contrary still regard "public ownership" as "progressive" and resist every effort to de-nationalize or privatize the economy.

It is true that today's increasingly liberalized global economy, uncritically hailed by the great multinational corporations, is itself unstable. It is also, alas, true that liberalization does not always result in automatic "trickle down" of benefits to the poor. Nevertheless, incontrovertible evidence proves that state-owned enterprises mistreat their employees, pollute the air and abuse the public at least as efficiently as private enterprises. Many have become sinkholes of inefficiency, corruption and greed. Their failures frequently encourage a vast, seething black market that undermines the very legitimacy of the state.

But worst and most ironic of all, instead of taking the lead in technological advance as promised, nationalized enterprises as a rule are almost uniformly reactionary—the most bureaucratic, the slowest to reorganize, the least willing to adapt to changing consumer needs, the most afraid to provide information to the citizen, the last to adopt advanced technology.

For more than a century, socialists and defenders of capitalism waged bitter war over public versus private property. Large numbers of men and women literally laid down their lives over this issue. What neither side imagined was a new wealth-creation system that would make virtually all their arguments obsolete.

Yet this is exactly what happened. For the most important form of property is now intangible. It is super-symbolic. It is knowledge. The same knowledge can be used by many people simultaneously to create wealth and to produce still more knowledge. And unlike factories and fields, knowledge is, for all intents, inexhaustible.

A second pillar in the cathedral of socialist theory was central planning. Instead of allowing the "chaos" of the marketplace to determine the economy, intelligent top-down planning would be able to concentrate resources on key sectors and accelerate technological development.

But central planning depended on knowledge, and as early as the 1920s the Austrian economist Ludwig von Mises identified its lack of knowledge or, as he termed it, its "calculation problem" as the Achilles heel of socialism.

How many shoes and what sizes should a factory in Irkutsk make? How many left-handed screws or grades of paper? What price-relationships should be set between carburetors and cucumbers? How many rubles, zlotys or yuan should be invested in each of tens of thousands of different lines and levels of production?

Generations of earnest socialist planners wrestled desperately with this knowledge problem. The planners demanded ever more data and got ever more lies from the managers afraid to report shortfalls in production. They beefed up the bureaucracy. Lacking the supply-and-demand signals generated by a competitive market, they tried measuring the economy in terms of labor hours, or counting things in terms of kind, rather than money. Later they tried econometric modeling and input-output analysis.

Nothing worked. The more information they had, the more complex and disorganized the economy grew. Fully three quarters of a century after the Russian Revolution, the real symbol of the U.S.S.R. was not the hammer and sickle but the consumer queue.

Today, all across the socialist and ex-socialist spectrum, there is a race to introduce market economics. Approaches vary, as do the attempts to provide a "safety net" for dislocated workers. But it is now almost universally recognized by socialist reformers that allowing supply and demand to determine prices (at least within certain ranges) provides what the central plan could not—price signals indicating what is or is not needed and wanted in the economy.

However, overlooked in the discussion among economists over the need for these signals is the fundamental change in communication pathways they imply, and the tremendous power shifts that changes in communication systems bring. The most important difference between centrally planned economies and market-driven economies is that in the first, information flows vertically, whereas in the market, much more in formation flows horizontally and diagonally in the system with buyers and sellers exchanging information at every level.

This change does not merely threaten top bureaucrats in the planning ministries and in management but millions upon millions of mini-bureaucrats whose sole source of power depends on their control of information fed up the reporting channel.

The new wealth-creation methods require so much knowledge, so much information and communication, that they are totally out of reach of centrally planned economies. The rise of the super-symbolic economy thus collides with a second foundation of socialist orthodoxy.

THE DUSTBIN OF HISTORY

The third crashing pillar of socialism was its overweening emphasis on hardware—its total concentration on smokestack industry and its derogation of both agriculture and mind work.

In the years after the 1917 revolution, the Soviets lacked capital to build all the steel mills, dams and auto plants they needed. Soviet leaders seized on the theory of "socialist primitive accumulation" formulated by the economist E. A. Preobrazhensky. This theory held that the necessary capital could be squeezed out of the peasants by forcing their standard of living down to an emaciating minimum and skimming off their surpluses. These would then be used to capitalize heavy industry and subsidize the workers.

As a result of this "industry bias," as the Chinese call it today, agriculture has been a disaster area for virtually all socialist economies and still is. Put differently, the socialist countries pursued a Second Wave strategy at the expense of their First Wave people.

But socialists also frequently denigrated the services and white-collar work. Because the goal of socialism everywhere was to industrialize as rapidly as possible, it was muscle labor that was glorified. This widespread attitude went hand in hand with the tremendous concentration on production rather than consumption, on capital goods rather than consumer goods.

Mainline Marxists typically held the materialist view that ideas, information, art, culture, law, theories and the other intangible products of the mind were merely part of a "superstructure" which hovered, as it were, over the economic base of society. While there was, admittedly, a certain feedback between the two, it was the base that determined the superstructure, rather than the reverse. Those who argued otherwise were condemned as "idealists"—at times a decidedly dangerous label to wear.

For Marxists, hardware was always more important than software. The computer revolution now teaches us that the opposite is true. If anything, it is knowledge that drives the economy, not the economy that drives knowledge.

Societies, however, are not machines, and they are not computers. They cannot be reduced so simply into hardware and software, base and superstructure. A more apt model would picture them as consisting of many elements all connected in immensely complex and continually changing feedback loops. As their complexity rises, knowledge becomes more central to both their economic and ecological survival.

In brief, the rise of a Third Wave economy whose primary raw material is in fact soft and intangible found world socialism totally unprepared. Socialism's collision with the future was fatal.

SEVEN

A COLLISION OF CONSTITUENCIES

The list of problems facing our own society is endless. We smell the moral rot of a dying industrial civilization as we watch its institutions, one after an other, collapse in a welter of ineffectuality and corruption. As a result, the air fills with bitterness and demands for radical change. In response, thousands of proposals are put forward, all claiming to be basic or fundamental or even revolutionary. Yet again and again, new rules, new laws, regulations, plans and practices, all intended to solve our problems, boomerang and make them worse, adding to the helpless feeling that nothing works. This feeling, which is extremely dangerous for any democracy, feeds the hunger for the proverbial "man on a white horse." Unless we are bold and imaginative, we, too, could find ourselves in "the dustbin of history."

American politics is presented to us by our media as a continuing gladiatorial contest between two political parties. Yet Americans are increasingly alienated, bored and angry at both the media and the politicians. Party politics seem to most people a kind of shadow-play, insincere, costly and corrupt. Increasingly, people ask: does it matter who wins?

The answer is yes—but not for the reasons we are usually given.

In 1980 in *The Third Wave*, we wrote:

. . . the most important political development of our time is the emergence in our midst of two basic camps, one committed to Second Wave civilization, the other to Third. One is tenaciously dedicated to preserving the core institutions of industrial mass society—the nuclear family, the mass education system, the giant corporation, the mass trade union, the centralized nation-state and the politics of pseudorepresentative government. The other recognizes that today's most urgent problems, from energy, war and poverty to ecological degradation and the breakdown of familial relationships, can no longer be solved within the framework of an industrial civilization.

The lines between these two camps are not yet sharply drawn. As individuals, most of us are divided, with a foot in each. Issues still appear murky and unconnected to one another. In addition, each camp is composed of many groups pursuing their own narrowly perceived self-interest, without any overarching vision. Nor does either side have a monopoly on moral virtue. There are decent people ranged on both sides. Nevertheless, the differences between these two subsurface political formations are enormous.

LOBBYING FOR THE PAST

The reason the public does not even now recognize the crucial importance of this cleavage is that too much of what the press covers is, in fact, the politics-as-usual conflict between different Second Wave groups over the spoils of the old system. Despite their differences, these Second Wave groups quickly coalesce to oppose Third Wave initiatives.

This is the reason why in 1984, when Gary Hart campaigned for the Democratic Party presidential nomination and won the New Hampshire primary by calling for "new thinking," the old Second Wave barons in the Democratic Party united to stop him and nominated solid, safe, Second Wave thinker Walter Mondale instead.

It is why, more recently, Second Wave Naderites and Second Wave Buchananites found common cause against NAFTA.

It is why, when Congress passed an infra-structure bill in 1991, $150 billion was allocated to roads, highways, bridges and potholes—providing profits to Second Wave companies and jobs for Second Wave—unions, while a mere $1 billion was allocated to help build the much-touted electronic superhighway. Necessary as they may be, roads and highways are part of the Second Wave infrastructure; digital networks are the heart of the Third Wave infrastructure. The point here is not whether or not the government should subsidize the digital network, but the imbalance of Second and Third Wave forces in Washington.

This imbalance is why Vice President Gore—with one toe wet in the Third Wave—has been unable, despite his efforts, to "reinvent" the government along Third Wave lines. Centralized bureaucracy is the quintessential form of organization in Second Wave societies. Even as advanced corporations, driven by competition, are desperately trying to dismantle their bureaucracies and invent new Third Wave forms of management, government agencies, blocked by Second Wave civil service unions, have managed to stay largely unreformed, unreengineered, unreinvented. They retain, in short, their Second Wave structures.

Second Wave elites fight to retain or reinstate an unsustainable past because they gained wealth and power from applying Second Wave principles, and the shift to a new way of life challenges that wealth and power. But it isn't only the elites. Millions of middle-class and poor Americans also resist the transition to the Third Wave because of an often justified fear that they will be left behind, will lose their jobs and slide further down the economic and social slope.

To understand the vast inertial power of Second Wave forces in America, however, we need to look beyond the old muscle-based industries and their workers and unions. The Second Wave sector is backed by those elements of Wall Street that service it. It is further supported by intellectuals and academics, often tenured, who live off grants from foundations, trade associations and lobbies that serve it. Their task is to collect supportive data and hammer out the ideological arguments and slogans used by Second Wave forces: for example, the idea that the information-intensive service industries are "unproductive," or that service workers are doomed to "sling hamburgers" or that the economy must revolve around manufacturing.

With all this firepower continually battering them, it is hardly surprising that both political parties reflect Second Wave thinking. The Democrats' reflexive reliance on bureaucratic and centralist solutions to problems like the health insurance crisis is drawn straight from Second Wave theories of efficiency. Despite an occasional politician like Vice President Gore, who recognizes the importance of high technology and who once served as Cochair of the Congressional Clearinghouse on the Future, the Democrats remain so heavily indebted to their Second Wave backers in industry, the unions and the civil service, that as a party, they remain largely paralyzed in the face of the twenty-first century.

From Hart in the '80s to Gore in the '90s, the party's core constituencies make it impossible for the Democratic Party to follow its most forward thinking leaders. The party thus finds itself still trapped by its blue-collar image of reality.

The failure of the Democrats to make themselves the party of the future (as indeed they once were) has thrown the door wide open for their adversaries. The Republicans are less rooted in the old industrial Northeast, and thus have an opportunity to position themselves as the party of the Third Wave—although their recent Presidents have signally failed to seize this opportunity. And the Republicans, too, rely on knee-jerk Second Wave rhetoric.

Republicans are basically right when they call for broad scale deregulation because businesses now need all the flexibility possible to survive global competition. Republicans are basically right in calling for privatization of government operations because governments, lacking competition, don't generally run things well. Republicans are basically right when they urge us to take maximum advantage of the dynamism and creativity that market economies make possible. But they, too, remain prisoners of Second Wave economics. For example, even the free-market economists on whom Republicans rely have failed, as yet, to come to terms with the new role and inexhaustibility of knowledge.

Republicans also are still beholden to some of the corporate dinosaurs of the Second Wave past and to their trade associations, lobbies and policy formulating "round tables."

Moreover, Republicans tend to play down potentially immense social dislocations that are likely to flow from any change as profound as the Third Wave. For example, as skills become obsolete overnight, large numbers of the middle class, including highly trained people, may well find themselves thrown out of work. California defense scientists and engineers are a chastening case in point.

Free-marketism and trickle-downism twisted into rigid theological dogma are inadequate responses to the Third Wave. A party facing the future should be warning of problems to come and suggesting preventative change. For example, today's media revolution will bring enormous benefits to the emerging Third Wave economy. But TV shopping and other electronic services might well slash the number of entry-level jobs in the traditional retail sector, precisely the place undereducated young people can get their start.

If free markets and democracy are to survive the great and turbulent transitions to come, politics must become anticipatory and preventive. Yet asking our political parties to think beyond the next election is hard and thankless work.

Instead, both parties are busy mainlining nostalgia into their constituents' veins. The Democrats, for example, until recent years, spoke of "reindustrializing" or "restoring" American industry to its period of greatness in the 1950s (in reality an impossible return to the Second Wave mass-production economy). The Republicans, meanwhile, appeal to nostalgia in their rhetoric about culture and values, as though one could return to the values and morality of the 1950s—a time before universal television, before the birth-control pill, before commercial jet aviation, satellites and home computers—without also returning to the mass industrial society of the Second Wave. One side still dreams of River Rouge, the other dreams of Ozzie and Harriet.

The religion-based wing of the Republican Party, seeking a return to "traditional" verities, blames liberals, humanists and Democrats for the "collapse of morality." It fails to grasp that this crisis in our value system reflects the more general crisis of Second Wave civilization as a whole, and that this upheaval is not limited to America. Rather than asking how to bring about a decent, moral and democratic Third Wave America, most of its leaders merely urge a return to an idealized past. Instead of asking how to make a de-massified society moral and fair, many give the impression that they really want to re-massify America.

The difference between the parties, however, is that while the Second Wave "nostalgia pushers" in the Democratic Party are concentrated in its core constituencies, their counterparts in the Republican Party tend to be found on its frenetic fringe. This leaves room for the center of the party, if it is inclusive and open to change, to seize the future—lock, stock and barrel. This is the message that Newt Gingrich, the Republican Speaker of the House of Representatives, has been trying, but so far with only limited success, to deliver to his own party. If Gingrich succeeds, and the Democrats remain chained to their pre-computer ideology, they could, for good or ill, be trampled in the political dust.

In 1980, Lee Atwater was a top political advisor to President Reagan. Later he became President Bush's jogging companion and campaign manager. Not long after Reagan was elected, Atwater passed out copies of our book The Third Wave to White House officials. He called to tell us, and we interviewed him at irregular intervals during the years that followed. In 1989 we saw Lee Atwater once more, not long before he died. At that final dinner we told him that, in our view, it was unfortunate for the country that the Democrats had no positive vision of a Third Wave America. Atwater agreed. To our surprise, he quickly added, "But neither do the Republicans." Neither party, he said, had a positive image of the future, "and that's why the campaigning is so negative." All of America is poorer for our bipartisan myopia.

TOMORROW'S CONSTITUENCY

However powerful Second Wave forces may seem today, their future is diminishing. At the start of the industrial era First Wave forces dominated society and political life. Rural elites seemed destined to dominate forever. But they did not. Had they done so, the industrial revolution would not have succeeded in transforming the world.

Today the world is changing again, and the overwhelming majority of Americans are neither farmers nor factory workers. Instead, they are engaged in one or another form of knowledge work. America's fastest growing and most important industries are information-intensive, and the Third Wave sector includes more than high-flying computer and electronics firms and biotech start-ups. It embraces advanced, information-driven manufacturing in every industry. It includes the increasingly data-drenched services—finance, software, entertainment, the media, advanced communications, medical services, consulting, training and education. In short, it includes all the industries based on mind-work rather than muscle-work. The people who work in this sector will soon be the dominant constituency in American politics.

Unlike the "masses" during the industrial age, the rising Third Wave constituency is highly diverse. It is de-massified. It is composed of individuals who prize their differences. Its very heterogeneity contributes to its lack of political awareness. It is far harder to unify than the masses of the past.

Thus the Third Wave constituency has yet to develop its own think tanks and political ideology. It has not systematically marshaled support from academia. Its various associations and lobbies in Washington are still comparatively new and less well connected. And except for one issue, NAFTA, in which the Second Wavers were defeated, the new constituency has few significant notches on its legislative belt.

Yet there are key issues on which this broad constituency-to-come can agree. To start with: liberation. Liberation from all the old Second Wave rules, regulations, taxes and laws laid in place to serve the smokestack barons and bureaucrats of the past. These arrangements, no doubt sensible when Second Wave industry was the heart of the American economy, today obstruct Third Wave development.

For example, depreciation tax schedules lobbied into being by the old manufacturing interests presuppose that machines and products last for many years. Yet in the fast-changing high-tech industries, and particularly in the computer industry, their usefulness is measured in months or weeks. The result is a tax bias against high tech. Research and development deductions also favor big, old Second Wave companies over the dynamic start-ups on which the Third Wave sector depends. The current tax treatment of intangibles means that a company with a lot of obsolete sewing machines may well be favored over a software firm that has very little in the way of physical assets. (Even accounting standards, set not by government but by the Financial Accounting Standards Board, favor investment in hardware over information, human resources and other intangibles on which Third Wave companies depend.) Yet changing such rules will mean winning a bitter political fight against the Second Wave firms that benefit from them.

Companies in the Third Wave sector have special characteristics. They tend to be young—both in corporate age and in the age of their work force. Work units in them tend to be small compared with those in Second Wave firms. They tend to invest more than average in research and development, training, education and human resources. Ferocious competition forces them to innovate continuously. That means short product life-cycles, and it often implies a rapid turnover of people, tools and administrative practices. The key assets of these firms are symbols inside the skulls of their people. Should these firms and industries be expected to play the game according to rules that penalize them for precisely their Third Wave characteristics? Isn't this tying America's hands behind its back?

Much of the Third Wave Sector is engaged in providing a dazzling, ever-changing array of services. Instead of decrying the rise of the service sector and continually attacking it as a source of low productivity, low wages and low performance, shouldn't it be expressly supported and expanded? Shouldn't it at least be freed of old shackles? America needs more, not less, service sector employment to improve the quality of life of its people. That means jobs for everyone from electronics repairmen to recyclers, from health-care providers and people who help the elderly to police and firefighters, and—yes—it even means jobs for child-care providers and for domestic workers who are desperately needed in millions of two-income homes. A Third Wave economic policy should not pick winners and losers, but it should clear away the obstacles to professionalization and development of the services needed to make life in America less stressed-out, less frustrating and impersonal. Yet no political party as yet has even begun to think this way.

Despite this political lag, the Third Wave constituency is growing in power every day. Increasingly, it expresses itself outside the conventional political parties because neither party has so far noticed its existence. Thus it is Third Wavers who fill the ranks of the ever more numerous and potent grassroots organizations around the country. It is Third Wavers who dominate the new electronic communities springing up around the Internet. And it is these same people who are busy de-massifying the Second Wave media and creating an interactive alternative to it. Traditional party politicians who ignore these new realities will be swept aside like M.P.s in nineteenth-century England who imagined their rural, "rotten borough" seats in Parliament were permanently secure.

The Third Wave forces in America have yet to find their voice. The political party that gives it to them will dominate the American future. When that happens, a new and dramatically different America will rise from the ruins of the late-twentieth century.

EIGHT

PRINCIPLES FOR A THIRD WAVE AGENDA

With powerful changes swirling around us and demanding ever quicker responses, it often feels as though we are swimming faster and faster against a huge, unstoppable tide. And too often we are. Perhaps, like the surfer, we should use the energy of the wave itself to carry us forward.

The Third Wave we have described could carry America toward a better, more civil, more decent and democratic future. But it won't unless we distinguish between Second Wave and Third Wave economic, political and social policies. Our failure to make this critical distinction explains why so many well-intentioned innovations only seem to make matters worse.

We are living through the birth pangs of a new civilization whose institutions are not yet in place. A fundamental skill needed by policy makers, politicians and politically active citizens today—if they really want to know what they are doing—is the ability to distinguish between proposals designed to keep the tottering Second Wave system on life-support from those that spread and smooth our transition to the Third Wave civilization.

Here are some ways to tell which proposals are which.

1. DOES IT RESEMBLE A FACTORY?

The *factory* became the central symbol of industrial society. It became, in fact, a model for most other Second Wave institutions. Yet the factory as we have known it is fading into the past. Factories embody such principles as standardization, centralization, maximization, concentration and bureaucratization. Third Wave production is post-factory production based on new principles. It occurs in facilities that bear little resemblance to factories. In fact, an increasing amount is done in homes and offices, cars and planes.

The easiest and quickest way to spot a Second Wave proposal, whether in Congress or in a corporation, is to see whether it is still, consciously or not, based on the factory model.

America's schools, for example, still operate like factories. They subject the raw material (children) to standardized instruction and routine inspection. An important question to ask of any proposed educational innovation is simply this: is it intended to make the factory run more efficiently, or is it designed, as it should be, to get rid of the factory model altogether and replace it with individualized, customized education? A similar question could be asked of health legislation, welfare legislation and of every proposal to reorganize the federal bureaucracy. America needs new institutions built on post-bureaucratic, post-factory models.

If a proposal merely seeks to improve factory-style operations or to create a new factory, it may be a lot of things. The one thing it is not is Third Wave.

2. DOES IT MASSIFY SOCIETY?

People who ran those factories in the brute-force economy of the past liked large numbers of predictable, interchangeable, don't-ask-why workers for their assembly lines. And as mass production, mass distribution, mass education, mass media, and mass entertainment spread through the society, the Second Wave also created the "masses."

Third Wave economies, by contrast, will require (and will tend to reward) a radically different kind of worker—one who thinks, questions, innovates and takes entrepreneurial risk, a worker who is not easily interchangeable. Put differently, it will favor individuality (which is not necessarily the same as individualism).

The new brain-force economy tends to generate social diversity. Computerized, customized production makes possible highly diverse life-styles. Just check the local Wal-Mart with its 110,000 different products, or check the wide choice of coffees now offered by Starbucks against the types sold in America only a few years ago. But it isn't just about things. Much more important, the Third Wave also de-massifies culture, values and morality. De-massified media carry many different, often competing messages into culture. There are not only more varied kinds of work, but also more different kinds of leisure, styles of art, and political movements. There are more diverse religious belief systems. And in multiethnic America, there are also more distinct national, linguistic and sociocultural groups.

Second Wavers want to retain or restore the mass society. Third Wavers want to figure out how to make de-massification work for us.

3. HOW MANY EGGS IN THE BASKET?
The diversity and complexity of Third Wave society blow the circuits of highly centralized organizations. Concentrating power at the top was, and still is, a classic Second Wave way to try to solve problems. But, while centralization is sometimes needed, today's lop-sided over-centralization puts too many decisional eggs in one basket. The result is "decision overload." Thus in Washington today Congress and the White House are racing each other, trying to make too many decisions about too many fast changing, complex things that they know less and less about.

Third Wave organizations, by contrast, push as many decisions as possible down from the top and out to the periphery.

Companies are hurrying to empower employees, not out of altruism but because the people on the bottom often have better information and typically respond faster than the big shots on top to both crises and opportunities.

Putting eggs in many baskets, instead of all in one, is hardly a new idea, but it is one that Second Wavers hate.

4. IS IT VERTICAL OR VIRTUAL?

Second Wave organizations accumulate more and more functions over time and get fat. Third Wave organizations, instead of adding functions, subtract or subcontract them to stay slim. As a result, they outrace the dinosaurs when the Ice Age approaches.

Second Wave organizations find it hard to suppress the impulse toward "vertical integration"—the idea that to make a car you also have to mine the iron ore, ship it to the steel mill, make the steel, and ship it to the auto plant. Third Wave companies, by contrast, contract out as many of their tasks as possible, often to smaller more specialized high-tech companies and even to individuals who can do the work faster, better and cheaper. Carried to its limit, the corporation is deliberately hollowed out, its staff reduced to a minimum, its activities carried out at dispersed locations, the organization itself becoming what Oliver Williamson of Berkeley has called a "nexus of contracts." Charles Handy at the London Business School has argued that these "minimalist, partly unseen organizations" are now the "linchpins of our world."

While many of us may not work for them directly, we will, Handy notes, be selling our services to them and "the wealth of our societies will depend on them." Handy and Williamson are not alone in describing this radical new form of "virtual" organization made possible by Third Wave information and communication technologies.

Heidi Toffler, coauthor of this and all the original works capsuled in this volume, has introduced the important idea of "congruence"—that there must be some compatibility between the way the private sector and the public sector are organized if they aren't to stifle one another. Today the private sector is charging ahead on a supersonic jet. The public sector hasn't even unloaded its bags at the airport entry.

Evaluating a policy or program? Ask who is supposed to carry it out—verticalizers or virtualizers. The answer will provide a clue to whether it merely prolongs the unworkable past or helps introduce the future.

5. DOES IT EMPOWER THE HOME?

Before the industrial revolution, the family was large, and life revolved around the home. Home was where work took place, where the sick were tended and where the children were educated. It was the center of family entertainment. It was the place where the elderly were cared for. In First Wave societies, the large, extended family was the center of the social universe.

The decline of the family as a powerful institution did not begin with Dr. Spock or Playboy magazine. It began when the industrial revolution stripped most of these functions out of the family. Work shifted to the factory or office. The sick went off to hospitals, kids to schools, couples to movie theaters. The elderly went into nursing homes. What remained when all these tasks were exteriorized was the "nuclear family," held together less by the functions its members performed as a unit than by fragile psychological bonds that are all too easily snapped.

The Third Wave re-empowers the family and the home. It restores many of the lost functions that once made the home so central to society. An estimated thirty million Americans now do some part of their work at home, often using computers, faxes and other Third Wave technologies. Many parents are now choosing to home-school their kids, but the real change will come when computers-cum-television hit the household and are incorporated into the educational process. As to the sick? More and more medical functions, from pregnancy testing to checking blood pressure—tasks once done in hospitals or doctors' offices—are migrating back to the home. All this points to a stronger, not a weaker, home and to a stronger role for families– but families of many diverse types, some nuclear, some extended and multigenerational, some composed of remarrieds, some big, some small or childless, some in which the couple defers having children until later in life. This diversity of family structure reflects the diversity we find in the economy and culture as Second Wave mass society de-massifies.

The irony is that many "family values" advocates, without knowing it, are not pushing toward a stronger family when they urge a return to the nuclear household: they are trying to restore the standardized model of the Second Wave. If we really want to strengthen family and make the home a central institution again, we must forget peripheral issues, accept diversity, and return important tasks to the household—oh, yes, and make sure the parent keeps control of the remote.

* * * *

America is where the future usually happens first. If we are suffering from the crash of our old institutions, we are also pioneering a new civilization. That means living with high uncertainty. It means expecting disequilbria and upset. And it means no one has the full and final truth about where we are going—or even where we should go.

We need to feel our way, leaving no group behind, as we create the future in our midst. These few criteria can help us separate policies rooted in the Second Wave past from those that can help ease the way to our Third Wave future. The danger of any list of criteria, however, is that some people will be tempted to apply them literally, mechanically, even fanatically. And that is the opposite of what is required.

Toleration for error, ambiguity and, above all, diversity, backed by a sense of humor and proportion, are survival necessities as we pack our kit for the amazing trip into the next millennium. Get ready for what could be the most exciting ride in history.

TWENTY-FIRST-CENTURY DEMOCRACY

To the Founding Parents:

You are the revolutionists dead. You are the men and women, the farmers, merchants, artisans, lawyers, printers, pamphleteers, shopkeepers and soldiers who together created a new nation on the distant shores of America. You include the fifty-five who came together in 1787 to hammer out, during a broiling summer in Philadelphia, that astonishing document called the Constitution of the United States. Listening to the distant sounds of tomorrow, you sensed that a civilization was dying and a new one was being born. You are the inventors of a future that became our present.

That piece of paper, with the Bill of Rights added in 1791, is clearly one of the stunning achievements of human history. We conclude you were driven to it—were compelled, carried along by the tidal force of events, fearing the collapse of an ineffective government paralyzed by inappropriate principles and obsolete structures.

Even now your principles move us, as they have moved countless millions around the planet. It is difficult for us to read certain passages of Jefferson or Paine, for example, without being brought to the edge of tears by their beauty and meaning.

We thank you, the revolutionary dead, for having made possible our lives as American citizens under a government of laws, not men, and particularly for that precious Bill of Rights, which has

89

made it possible for us to think, to express unpopular views, however foolish or mistaken at times—indeed we write what follows without fear of suppression. Precisely because you lived between two civilizations—an old agricultural world already stirring with intimations of the industrial world to come—you understood the concept of political obsolescence.

You would have understood why even the Constitution of the United States needs to be reconsidered and altered—not to cut the federal budget or to embody this or that narrow principle, but to expand its Bill of Rights, taking account of threats to freedom unimagined in the past, and to create a whole new structure of government capable of making intelligent, democratic decisions necessary for our survival in a Third Wave, twenty-first-century America.

We come with no easy blueprint for tomorrow's constitution. We mistrust those who think they already have the answers when we are still trying to formulate the questions. But the time has come for us to imagine completely novel alternatives, to discuss, dissent, debate, and design from the ground up the democratic architecture of tomorrow.

Not in a spirit of anger or dogmatism, not in a sudden impulsive spasm, but through the widest consultation and peaceful public participation, we need to join together to reconstitute America.

You would have understood this need. For it was one of your generation—Jefferson—who, in mature reflection, declared, "Some men look at constitutions with sanctimonious reverence and deem them like the ark of the covenant, too sacred to be touched. They ascribe to the men of the preceding age a wisdom more than human and suppose what they did to be beyond amendment. . . . We are certainly not advocates for frequent and untried changes in laws and constitutions . . . but we also know that laws and institutions must go hand in hand with the progress of the human mind. . . . As new discoveries are made, new truths disclosed, and manners and opinions change with the change of circumstances, institutions must advance also, and keep pace with the times."

ALVIN AND HEIDI TOFFLER

For this wisdom above all, we thank Mr. Jefferson, who helped create the system that served us so well for so long and that now must, in its turn, die and be replaced.
Alvin and Heidi Toffler

An imaginary letter . . . Surely in many nations there must be others who, given the opportunity, would express similar sentiments. For the obsolescence of many of today's governments is not some secret we alone have discovered. Nor is it a disease of America alone.

The fact is that building a Third Wave civilization on the wreckage of Second Wave institutions involves the design of new, more appropriate political structures in many nations at once. This is a painful yet necessary project that is mind-staggering in scope and will no doubt take decades to complete.

In all likelihood it will require a protracted battle to radically overhaul the United States Congress, the House of Commons and the House of Lords, the French Chamber of Deputies, the Bundestag, the Diet, the giant ministries and entrenched civil services of many nations, their constitutions and court systems—in short, much of the unwieldy and increasingly unworkable apparatus of existing representative governments.

Nor will this wave of political struggle stop at the national level. Over the months and decades ahead, the entire "global law machine"—from the United Nations at one end to the local city or town council at the other—will eventually face a mounting, ultimately irresistible demand for restructuring.

All these structures will have to be fundamentally altered, not because they are inherently evil or even because they are controlled by this or that class or group, but because they are increasingly unworkable—no longer fitted to the needs of a radically changed world.

To build workable governments anew—and to carry out what may well be the most important political task of our lifetimes—

we will have to strip away the accumulated clichés of the Second Wave era. And we will have to rethink political life in terms of three key principles.

Indeed, these may well turn out to be the root principles of the Third Wave governments of tomorrow.

MINORITY POWER

The first, heretical principle of Third Wave government is that of minority power. It holds that majority rule, the key legitimating principle of the Second Wave era, is increasingly obsolete. It is not majorities but minorities that count. And our political systems must increasingly reflect that fact.

Expressing the beliefs of his revolutionary generation, it was Jefferson, once again, who asserted that governments must behave with "absolute acquiescence in the decisions of the majority." The United States and Europe—still at the dawn of the Second Wave era—were just beginning the long process that would turn them eventually into industrial mass societies. The concept of majority rule perfectly fit the needs of these societies. Our present mass democracy is the political expression of a mass production, mass consumption, mass education, mass media, mass society.

Today, as we have seen, we are leaving industrialism behind and rapidly becoming a de-massified society. In consequence it is growing increasingly difficult—often impossible—to mobilize a majority or even a governing coalition. In the United States, says political scientist Walter Dean Burnham of the Massachusetts Institute of Technology, "I don't see the basis for any positive majority on anything today."

In place of a highly stratified society in which a few major blocs ally themselves to form a majority, we have a configurative society—one in which thousands of minorities, many of them temporary, swirl and form highly novel, transient patterns, seldom coalescing into a consensus on major issues. The advance of Third Wave civilization thus weakens the very legitimacy of many existing governments.

The Third Wave also challenges all of our conventional assumptions about the relationship of majority rule to social justice. Throughout the era of Second Wave civilization the fight for majority rule was humane and liberating. In still-industrializing countries, like South Africa today, it remains so. In Second Wave societies, majority rule almost always meant a fairer break for the poor. For the poor were the majority.

Today however, in countries shaken by the Third Wave, precisely the opposite is often the case. The truly poor no longer necessarily have numbers on their side. In a good many countries they—like everyone else—have become a minority.

Not only is majority rule therefore no longer adequate as a legitimating principle, it is no longer necessarily humanizing or democratic in societies moving into the Third Wave.

Second Wave ideologues routinely lament the breakup of mass society. Rather than seeing in this enriched diversity an opportunity for human development, they attack it as "fragmentation" and "Balkanization" and attribute it to the aroused "selfishness" of minorities. This trivial explanation substitutes effect for cause. For the rising activism of minorities is not the result of a sudden onset of selfishness; it is, among other things, a reflection of the needs of a new system of production which requires for its very existence a far more varied, colorful, open and diverse society than any we have ever known.

We can either resist the thrust toward diversity, in a futile last-ditch effort to save our Second Wave political institutions, or we can acknowledge diversity and change those institutions accordingly.

The former strategy can only be implemented by totalitarian means and must result in economic and cultural stagnation; the latter leads toward social evolution and a minority-based, twenty-first-century democracy.

To reconstitute democracy in Third Wave terms, we need to jettison the frightening but false assumption that increased diversity automatically brings increased tension and conflict in society. Indeed, the exact reverse can be true. Conflict in society is not only necessary, it is, within limits, desirable. If one hundred men all desperately want the same brass ring, they may be forced to fight for it. On the other hand, if each of the hundred has a different objective, it is far more rewarding for them to trade, cooperate and form symbiotic relationships. Given appropriate social arrangements, diversity can make for a secure and stable civilization.

It is the lack of appropriate political institutions today that unnecessarily sharpens conflict between minorities to the knife-edge of violence. It is the lack of such institutions that makes minorities intransigent. It is the absence of such institutions that makes the majority harder and harder to find.

The answer to these problems is not to stifle dissent or to charge minorities with selfishness (as though the elites and their experts are not similarly self-interested). The answer lies in imaginative new arrangements for accommodating and legitimating diversity—new institutions that are sensitive to the rapidly shifting needs of changing and multiplying minorities.

Some day future historians may look back on voting and the search for majorities as an archaic ritual engaged in by communicational primitives. Today however, in a dangerous world, we cannot afford to delegate total power to anyone, we cannot surrender even the weak popular influence that exists under majoritarian systems, and we cannot allow tiny minorities to make vast decisions that tyrannize all other minorities.

This is why we must drastically revise the crude Second Wave methods by which we pursue the elusive majority. We need new approaches designed for a democracy of minorities—methods whose purpose is to reveal differences rather than to paper them over with forced or fake majorities based on exclusionary voting, sophistic framing of the issues or rigged electoral procedures. We need, in short, to modernize the entire system so as to strengthen the role of diverse minorities, yet permit them to form majorities.

In Second Wave societies, voting to determine the popular will provided an important source of intermittent feedback for the ruling elites. When conditions for one reason or another became intolerable for the majority, and fifty-one percent of the voters registered their pain, the elites could, at a minimum, shift parties, alter policies, or make some other accommodations.

Even in yesterday's mass society, however, the fifty-one percent principle was a decidedly blunt, purely quantitative instrument. Voting to determine the majority tells us nothing about the quality of people's views. It can tell us how many people at a given moment want X, but not how badly they want it. Above all, it tells us nothing about what they would be willing to trade off for X— crucial information in a society made up of many minorities.

Nor does it signal us when a minority feels so threatened or attaches such life-and-death significance to a single issue that its views should perhaps receive more than ordinary weight.

In a mass society these well-known weaknesses of majority rule were tolerated because, among other things, most minorities lacked strategic power to disrupt the system. In today's finely wired society, in which all of us are members of minority groups, that is no longer true.

For a de-massified Third Wave society the feedback systems of the industrial past are entirely too crude. Thus we will have to use voting and the polls in a radically new way.

Fortunately, Third Wave technologies provide pathways toward Third Wave democracy. They reopen, in a startling new context, fundamental issues that our founders considered two hundred years ago. These technologies make possible new, hitherto impractical forms of democracy.

The second building block of tomorrow's political systems must be the principle of "semidirect democracy"—a shift from depending on representatives to representing ourselves. The mixture of the two is semidirect democracy.

The collapse of consensus, as we have already seen, subverts the very concept of representation. Without agreement among the voters back home, whom does a representative really "represent"? At the same time, legislators have come to rely increasingly on staff support and on outside experts for advice in shaping the laws. British M.P.s are notoriously weak *vis-à-vis* the Whitehall bureaucracy because they lack adequate staff support, thus shifting more power away from Parliament to the unelected civil service.

The United States Congress, in an effort to counterbalance the influence of the executive bureaucracy, has created its own bureaucracy—a Congressional Budget Office, an Office of Technology Assessment and other necessary agencies and appendages. But this has merely transferred the problem from extramural to intramural. Our elected representatives know less and less about the myriad measures on which they must decide and are compelled to rely more and more on the judgment of others. The representative no longer even represents him or herself.

More basically, parliaments, congresses or assemblies were places in which, theoretically, the claims of rival minorities could be reconciled. Their representatives could make trade-offs for them. With today's blunt-edged Second Wave political tools, no legislator can even keep track of the many grouplets he or she nominally represents, let alone broker or trade effectively for them. And the more overloaded the American Congress or the German Bundestag or the Norwegian Storting becomes, the worse this situation grows.

This helps explain why single-issue political pressure groups become intransigent. Seeing limited opportunity for sophisticated trading or reconciliation through Congress or the legislatures, their demands on the system become non-negotiable. The theory of representative government as the ultimate broker collapses too.

The breakdown of bargaining, the decision crunch, the worsening paralysis of representative institutions mean, over the long term, that many of the decisions now made by small numbers of pseudo representatives may have to be shifted back gradually to the electorate itself. If our elected brokers can't make deals for us, we shall have to do it ourselves. If the laws they make are increasingly remote from or unresponsive to our needs, we shall have to make our own. For this, however, we shall need new institutions and new technologies as well.

The Second Wave revolutionaries who invented today's basic institutions were well aware of the possibilities of direct as against representative democracy. American revolutionists knew all about New England town halls and small-scale organic consensus formation. But the shortcomings and limitations of direct democracy were also well-known and, at that time, more persuasive.

"In *The Federalist* two objections to such an innovation were raised," write McCauley, Rood and Johnson, authors of a proposal for a National Plebiscite in the United States. "First, direct democracy allowed for no check or delay on temporary and emotional public reactions. And second, the communications of that day could not handle the mechanics."

These are legitimate problems. How would a frustrated and inflamed American public in the mid-1960s, for example, have voted on whether or not to drop a nuclear bomb on Hanoi? Or a West German public, furious at the Baader-Meinhof terrorists, on a proposal to set up camps for "sympathizers"? What if Canadians had held a plebiscite over Quebec the week after Rene Levesque took power? Elected representatives are presumed to be less emotional and more deliberative than the public.

The problem of overly motional public response, however, can be overcome in various ways, such as requiring a cooling-off period or second vote before implementation of major decisions taken via referendum or other forms of direct democracy.

The other objection can also be met. For the old communication limitations no longer stand in the way of expanded direct democracy. Today's spectacular advances in communications technology open for the first time a mind-boggling array of possibilities for direct citizen participation in political decision-making.

Years ago we had the pleasure of keynoting an historic event—the world's first "electronic town hall"—over the Qube cable TV system in Columbus, Ohio. Using this interactive communications system, residents of a small Columbus suburb actually took part via electronics in a political meeting of their local planning commission. By pushing a button in their living rooms, they were able to vote instantly on proposals relating to such practical issues as local zoning, housing codes and proposed highway construction. They were able not only to vote yes or no, but to participate in the discussion and speak up on the air. They were even able by push button to tell the chairperson when to move on to the next point on the agenda.

This was only a first, most primitive indication of tomorrow's potential for direct democracy. Using today's far more advanced computers, satellites, telephones, cable, polling techniques and other tools, not to mention the Internet and other communications networks, an educated citizenry can for the first time in history begin making many of its own political decisions.

This is not an either/or issue. It is not a question of "electronic town halls" in the crude form referred to by Ross Perot. Far more sensitive and sophisticated democratic processes are possible. And it is certainly not a question of direct democracy *versus* indirect, representation by self *versus* representation by others.

Many imaginative arrangements can be invented to *combine*

direct and indirect democracy. Right now members of Congress and most other parliaments or legislatures set up their own committees. There is no way for citizens to force lawmakers to create a committee to deal with some neglected or highly controversial issue. But why couldn't voters be empowered directly through petition to compel a legislative body to set up committees on topics the public—not the lawmakers—deems important?

We hammer away at such "blue-sky" proposals not because we unhesitatingly favor them but merely to underscore the more general point: there are powerful ways to open and democratize a system that is now near breakdown and in which few, if any, feel adequately represented. But we must begin thinking outside the worn grooves of the past three hundred years. We can no longer solve our problems with the ideologies, the models, or the leftover structures of the Second Wave past.

Fraught with uncertain implications, such novel proposals warrant careful local experimentation before we apply them on a broad scale. But however we may feel about this or that suggestion, the old objections to direct democracy are growing weaker at precisely the time that the objections to representative democracy are growing stronger. Dangerous or even bizarre as it may seem to some, semidirect democracy is a moderate principle that can help us design workable new institutions for the future.

DECISION DIVISION

Opening the system to more minority power and allowing citizens to play a more direct role in their own governance are both necessary, but carry us only part of the way. The third vital principle for the politics of tomorrow is aimed at breaking up the decisional logjam and putting decisions where they belong. This, not simply reshuffling leaders, is the antidote to political paralysis. We call it "decision division."

Some problems cannot be solved on a local level. Others

cannot be solved on a national level. Some require action at many levels simultaneously. Moreover, the appropriate place to solve a problem doesn't stay put. It changes over time.

To cure today's decision logjam, resulting from institutional overload, we need to divide up the decisions and reallocate them—sharing them more widely and switching the site of decision-making as the problems themselves require.

Today's political arrangements violate this principle wildly. The problems have shifted, but the decisional power hasn't. Thus, too many decisions are still concentrated, and the institutional architecture is most elaborate at the national level. By contrast, not enough decisions are being made at the transnational level, and the structures needed there are radically underdeveloped. In addition, too few decisions are left for the subnational level—regions, states, provinces and localities, or non-geographical social groupings.

At the transnational level, we are as politically primitive and underdeveloped today as we were at the national level when the industrial revolution began three hundred years ago. By transferring some decisions "up" from the nation-state, we not only make it possible to act effectively at the level where many of our most explosive problems lie, but simultaneously reduce the decision burden at the overloaded center—the nation-state. Decision division is essential.

But moving decisions up the scale is only half the task. It is also clearly necessary to move a vast amount of decision-making downward from the center.

Again the issue is not "either/or" in character. It is not decentralization versus centralization in some absolute sense. The issue is rational reallocation of decision-making in a system that has overstressed centralization to the point at which new information flows are swamping the central decision-makers.

Political decentralization is no guarantee of democracy—quite vicious localist tyrannies are possible. Local politics are frequently even more corrupt than national politics. Moreover, much that passes for decentralization is a kind of pseudo-decentralization for the benefit of the centralizers.

Nevertheless, with all these caveats, there is no possibility of restoring sense, order and management "efficiency" to many governments without a substantial devolution of central power. We need to divide the decision load and shift a significant part of it downward.

This is not because romantic anarchists want us to restore "village democracy" or because angry affluent taxpayers want to cut back on welfare services to the poor. The reason is that any political structure—even with banks of computers—can handle only so much information and no more, can produce only a certain quantity and quality of decisions, and that the decisional implosion has now pushed governments beyond this breakpoint.

Moreover, the institutions of government must correlate with the structure of the economy, the information system and other features of the civilization. Today we are witnessing a fundamental decentralization and regionalism of production and economic activity. Indeed it may well be that the basic unit is no longer the national economy.

What we are seeing, as we have already stressed elsewhere, is the emergence of very large, more and more cohesive regional sub-economies within each national economy. At the corporate level, we not only see efforts at internal decentralization but an actual geographical decentralization as well.

All this reflects, in part, a gigantic shift of information flows in society. We are, as noted earlier, undergoing a fundamental de-massification of communications as the power of the central networks wanes. We are seeing a stunning proliferation of cable, cassette, computer and private electronic mail systems, all pushing in the same decentralist direction.

It is not possible for a society to de-massify economic activity, communications and many other crucial processes without also, sooner or later, being compelled to decentralize government decision-making as well.

All this demands more than cosmetic changes in existing political institutions. It implies massive battles over control of budgets, taxes, land, energy and other resources. Decision division will not come easily, but it is absolutely unavoidable in country after overcentralized country.

THE EXPANDING ELITES

The concept of "decision load" is crucial to any understanding of democracy. All societies require a certain quantity and quality of political decisions in order to function. Indeed each society has its own unique decision structure. The more numerous, varied, frequent and complex the decisions required to run it, the heavier its political decision load. And the way this load is shared fundamentally influences the level of democracy in society.

In preindustrial societies, where the division of labor was rudimentary and change was slow, the number of political or administrative decisions actually required to keep things running was minimal. The decision load was small. A tiny, semi-educated, unspecialized feudal or monarchical elite could more or less run things without help from below, carrying the entire decision load by itself.

What we now call democracy burst forth only when the decision load suddenly swelled beyond the capacity of the old elite to handle it. The arrival of the Second Wave, bringing expanded trade, a greater division of labor and a leap to a whole new level of complexity in society, caused the same kind of decision implosion in its time that the Third Wave is causing today.

As a result, the decisional capabilities of the old ruling groups were overwhelmed, and new elites and sub-elites had to be recruited to cope with the decision load. Revolutionary new political institutions had to be designed for that purpose.

As industrial society developed, becoming ever more complex, its integrating elites, the "technicians of power," were in their turn continually compelled to recruit new blood to help them carry the expanding decision load. It was this invisible but inexorable process that drew the middle class more and more into the political arena. It was this expanded need for decision-making that led to an ever wider franchise and created more niches to be filled from below.

If this picture is even roughly correct, it tells us that the extent of democracy depends less on culture, less on Marxist class, less on battlefield courage, less on rhetoric, less on political will, than on the decision load of any society. A heavy load will ultimately have to be shared through wider democratic participation. So long as the decision load of the social system expands, therefore, democracy becomes not a matter of choice but of evolutionary necessity. The system cannot run without it.

What all this further suggests is that we may well be on the edge of another great democratic leap forward. For the very implosion of decision-making now overwhelming our presidents, prime ministers and governments unlocks—for the first time since the industrial revolution—exciting prospects for a radical expansion of political participation.

The need for new political institutions exactly parallels our need for new family, educational and corporate institutions as well. It is deeply wired into our search for a new energy base, new technologies and new industries. It reflects the upheaval in communications and the need to restructure relationships with the non-industrial world. It is, in short, the political reflection of accelerating changes in all these different spheres.

Without seeing these connections, it is impossible to make sense of the headlines around us. For today the single most important political conflict is no longer between rich and poor, between top-dog and underdog ethnic groups or even between capitalism and socialist visions. The decisive struggle today is between those who try to prop up and preserve industrial society and those who are ready to advance beyond it. This is the super struggle for tomorrow.

A DESTINY TO CREATE

Some generations are born to create, others to maintain a civilization. The generations who launched the Second Wave of historic change were compelled, by force of circumstance, to be creators. The Montesquieus, Mills and Madisons invented most of the political forms we still take for granted. Caught between two civilizations, it was their destiny to create.

Today in every sphere of social life, in our families, our schools, our businesses and churches, in our energy systems and communications, we face the need to create new Third Wave forms, and millions of people in many countries are already beginning to do so. Nowhere, however, is obsolescence more advanced or more dangerous than in our political life. And in no field today do we find less imagination, less experiment, less willingness to contemplate fundamental change.

Even people who are daringly innovative in their own work—in their law offices or laboratories, their kitchens, classrooms, or companies—seem to freeze up at any suggestion that our Constitution or political structures are obsolete and in need of radical overhaul. So frightening is the prospect of deep political change with its attendant risks, that the status quo, however surrealistic and oppressive, suddenly seems like the best of all possible worlds.

Conversely we have in every society a fringe of pseudo-revolutionaries, steeped in obsolete Second Wave assumptions, for whom no proposed change is radical enough: archaeo-marxists, anarcho-romantics, right-wing fanatics, racist demagogues and religious zealots, armchair guerrillas and honest-to-God terrorists, dreaming of totalitarian technocracies, medieval utopias or theocratic states. Even as we speed into a new historical zone, they nurse dreams of revolution drawn from the yellowed pages of yesterday's political tracts.

Yet what lies ahead as the super struggle intensifies is not a replay of any previous revolutionary drama—no centrally directed overthrow of the ruling elites by some "vanguard party" with the masses in tow; no spontaneous, supposedly cathartic, mass uprising triggered by terrorism. The creation of new political structures for a Third Wave civilization will not come in a single climactic upheaval but as a consequence of a thousand innovations and collisions at many levels in many places over a period of decades.

This does not rule out the possibility of violence along the way to tomorrow. The transition from First Wave to Second Wave civilization was one long, blood-drenched drama of wars, revolts, famines, forced migrations, *coups d'état* and calamities. Today the stakes are much higher, the time shorter, the acceleration faster, the dangers even greater.

Much depends on the flexibility and intelligence of today's elites, sub-elites and super-elites. If these groups prove to be as shortsighted, unimaginative and frightened as most ruling groups in the past, they will rigidly resist the Third Wave and thereby escalate the risks of violence and their own destruction.

If, by contrast, they flow with the Third Wave, if they recognize the need for a broadened democracy, they in fact can join in the process of creating a Third Wave civilization, just as the most intelligent First Wave elites anticipated the coming of a technologically based industrial society and joined in its creation.

Circumstances differ from country to country, but never in history have there been so many reasonably educated people collectively armed with so incredible a range of knowledge. Never have so many enjoyed so high a level of affluence, precarious perhaps, yet ample enough to allow them time and energy for civic concern and action. Never have so many been able to travel, to communicate and to learn so much from other cultures. Above all, never have so many had so much to gain by guaranteeing that the necessary changes, though profound, be made peacefully.

Elites, no matter how enlightened, cannot by themselves make a new civilization. The energies of whole peoples will be required. But those energies are available, waiting to be tapped. Indeed if we, particularly in the high-technology countries, took as our explicit goal for the next generation the creation of wholly new institutions and constitutions, we could release something far more powerful even than energy: the collective imagination.

The sooner we begin to design alternative political institutions based on the three principles described above—minority power, semidirect democracy and decision division—the better our chances for a peaceful transition. It is the attempt to block such changes, not the changes themselves, that raises the level of risk. It is the blind attempt to defend obsolescence that creates the danger of bloodshed.

This means that to avoid violent upheaval we must begin now to focus on the problem of structural, political obsolescence around the world. And we must take this issue not merely to the experts, the constitutionalists, lawyers and politicians, but to the public itself—to civic organizations, trade unions, churches, to women's groups, to ethnic and racial minorities, to scientists and housewives and businessmen.

We must, as a first step, launch the widest possible public debate over the need for a new political system attuned to the needs of a Third Wave civilization. We need conferences, television programs, contests, simulation exercises, mock constitutional conventions to generate the broadest array of imaginative proposals for political restructuring, to unleash an outpouring of fresh ideas. We should be prepared to use the most advanced tools available to us, from satellites and computers to video discs and interactive television.

No one knows in detail what the future holds or what will work best in a Third Wave society. For this reason we should think not of a single massive reorganization or of a single revolutionary, cataclysmic change imposed from the top, but of thousands of conscious, decentralized experiments that permit us to test new models of political decision-making at local and regional levels in advance of their application to the national and transnational levels.

But, at the same time, we must also begin to build a constituency for similar experimentation—and radical redesign—of institutions at the national and transnational levels as well. Today's widespread disillusionment, anger and bitterness against the world's Second Wave governments can either be whipped into fanatic frenzy by demagogues calling for authoritarian leadership, or it can be mobilized for the process of democratic reconstruction.

By launching a vast process of social learning—an experiment in anticipatory democracy in many nations at once—we can head off the totalitarian thrust. We can prepare millions for the dislocations and dangerous crises that lie before us. And we can place strategic pressure on existing political systems to accelerate the necessary changes.

Without this tremendous pressure from below, we should not expect many of today's nominal leaders—presidents and politicians, senators and central committee members—to challenge the very institutions that, no matter how obsolete, give them prestige, money and the illusion, if not the reality, of power. Some unusual, farseeing politicians or officials will lend their early support to the struggle for political transformation. But most will move only when the demands from outside are irresistible or when the crisis is already so advanced and so close to violence that they see no alternative.

The responsibility for change, therefore, lies with us. We must begin with ourselves, teaching ourselves not to close our minds prematurely to the novel, the surprising, the seemingly radical. This means fighting off the idea-assassins who rush forward to kill any new suggestion on grounds of its impracticality, while defending whatever now exists as practical, no matter how absurd, oppressive, or unworkable it may be. It means fighting for freedom of expression—the right of people to voice their ideas, even if heretical.

Above all it means starting this process of reconstruction now, before the further disintegration of existing political systems sends the forces of tyranny jackbooting through the streets, and makes impossible a peaceful transition to twenty-first-century democracy.

If we begin now, we and our children can take part in the exciting reconstitution not merely of our obsolete political structures but of civilization itself.

Like the generation of the revolutionary dead, we have a destiny to create.

109

WHEN AUTHORS BRING together chapters from their earlier works, the result is often a collection of disparate ideas. That is decidedly not true of this book. While some of the chapters are drawn from previously published books, *Creating a New Civilization* is not an anthology. It is a fresh whole made possible by the modular character of our works, each of which is based on consciously designed models of accelerating social and political change. In this new form we believe we offer a primer, as it were, a key to our larger body of work.

Chapters one and nine were first published in 1980 in our book *The Third Wave*. Chapters two and four are taken from our most recent work, *War and Anti-War*, published in 1993. Chapters three, five and six come from *Powershift*, published in 1990. The versions presented here have been cut substantially from their originals but otherwise have been modified only slightly to provide logical transitions. By contrast, chapters seven and eight have never published before.

The idea for this volume initially came from Jeffrey A. Eisenach, President of the Progress & Freedom Foundation (Suite 550, 1250 H Street, N.W., Washington, D.C. 20005; Tel: 202/484-2312). Recognizing that Americans and their political leaders tend to look at each headline, each newsclip, each congressional battle and each technological breakthrough as a detached, independent event, Eisenach recognizes the political importance of synthesis. Moreover, he believes that the time for knee-jerk politics is over. With that in mind, he came to us with the proposal for this volume.

We thank him for doing so. We also wish to acknowledge the extremely helpful editorial assistance of Dr. Albert S. Hanser, a Senior Fellow at the Progress & Freedom Foundation, who surveyed the previously published materials from which this text is partly drawn and chose excerpts from them; and of Eric Michael, a Research Fellow who served as editorial assistant on the project.

We hope this book will help readers make the zero-base revaluation of their ideas that tomorrow's emergent civilization demands.

ALVIN AND HEIDI TOFFLER are among the world's most renowned social thinkers. Their books, including *Future Shock, The Third Wave, Powershift,* and *War and Anti-War,* are widely regarded as classics.

Future Shock was awarded the McKinsey Foundation Book Award for contributions to management literature. In France it won the prestigious Prix du Meilleur Livre Etranger. In China *The Third Wave,* was first banned as a bearer of "Western spiritual pollution," then published in the millions of copies and widely acclaimed as the "Bible" of the democratic reform movement just before the Tienanmen Square crackdown.

Alvin Toffler has been a Visiting Scholar at the Russell Sage Foundation, a Visiting Professor at Cornell University, a faculty member of the New School for Social Research, and a White House correspondent. He holds honorary doctorates in letters, law and science. He has been named an Officier de l'Ordre des Artes et Lettres in France and elected a Fellow of the American Association for the Advancement of Science.

Heidi Toffler has been, among other things, a union shop steward, a research librarian, and a TV documentary producer. Currently an Adjunct Professor at the National Defense University in Washington, she has been awarded, among other honors, the Medal of the President of the Italian Republic for her contributions to social thought.

The Tofflers are honorary cochairs of the U.S. Committee for UNIFEM, the United Nations Development Fund for Women. They have been married for forty-five years and have an adult daughter.